AIM
FOR THE
CHILDREN

Daniel E. Johnson

Aim for the Children
Copyright 1997 by Daniel E. Johnson

Printed in the United States of America

ISBN: 0-9651421-1-6

Unless otherwise noted, all Scripture quotations are from the *New King James Version.* Copyright 1979, 1980, 1982 by Thomas Nelson, Inc. Nashville, Tennessee. Scripture quotation marked NIV is from the *New International Version.* Copyright 1973, 1978, 1984, International Bible Society.

DEDICATION

To

Phillip
Lars
Chuckie
Corrine

A FATHER'S PRIDE

A MOTHER'S JOY

A NATION'S HOPE

ACKNOWLEDGMENTS

The following friends made publication of this book possible. Their generous participation is gratefully acknowledged:

Dr. and Mrs. Per A. Anderas
Bob and Chris Behrens
Nellie Bicksler
Gerald and Marjorie Boatsman
Alex and Eugenia Boryczewski
Samuel and Marvel Cline
David and Kathleen Curry
Rev. and Mrs. Robert Dearborn
Edith Denton
John and Cindy Duerr
Willard and Pat Dugger
Forest Hill Community Church — Memphis, Tennessee
Richard and Marlene Funk
Bruce and Gayla Gibbons
Sandy and Esther Glover
Shirley Hoder
Clarice Honeycutt

Nyal Hughes
Sam and Joyce Johnson
Bill and Judy Kingery
Hazel Lentz
Ruth Lunn
Jim and Marilynn Martin
Sharon Ruehle
Mary Louise Spillers
Ben and Saundra Steverson
Harold and Ginny Sweigart
Vlasta M. Vopalensky
Olga Waligunda

CONTENTS

PREFACE

Better sit down for this. There's more red meat here than pabulum.

A friend, then 70, found his whole world threatened. In defending himself, he cited his years of experience as reason for being heard and said, "I'm not 70 for nothing."

I'm not 70, but I have lived long enough to tell the difference between weeds and flowers, between good fruit and bad. I know the difference between the scent of perfume and the smell of garbage. And I'm quite tired of the garbage that has been strewn over the neighborhood, awaiting the footsteps of our children. Like land mines buried in the grass, a false step here or a false step there and limbs are flying and lives are lost.

And I am angry.

Angry, because the purveyors of garbage are both dishonest and cowardly: Dishonest because they say one thing and mean another; and cowardly because they prey upon the most vulnerable among us — the children.

Dishonest and cowardly, and I might add arrogant. At least that's the impression I got during my last visit to the headquarters of the National Education Association (NEA) in Washington, D.C. A simple request for information about their programs elicited an offer to be escorted out of the building.

What am I talking about? The attempt to reshape the United Stated of America by altering the attitudes, values, and beliefs of our children. The following chapters document the assault. Sinister and subtle in its inception, it became impudent and open in its implementation; still, it took us by surprise.

One of our Lord's parables includes a sentence worth pondering: "And while men slept, the enemy sowed tares." We were sleeping while history was being revised, deleting religion from our schools and booting God out of public life.

**We were . . . comatose when the state
took possession of our kids.**

Sixty of the most popular textbooks used in our public schools were examined by Dr. Paul C. Vitz, a New York University psychology professor. "The most striking thing about these texts," Dr. Vitz stated, "is the total absence of the Christian religion in them." Other beliefs were mentioned — the Jewish, Amish, Mormon, and Catholic faiths — "but little or no mention was made of the evangelical Protestants who founded this nation."[1]

We were slumbering when God became *persona non grata* in American life and caught napping when the education establishment was hijacked by an alien philosophy. We were in a deep sleep when classrooms were converted to clinics and teachers to therapists — and comatose when the state took possession of our kids.

Too strong an indictment? Then explain Professor John Goodlad's statement in *The NEA Journal:*

> The most controversial issues of the 21st century will pertain to the ends and means of modifying human behavior and who shall determine them. The first educational question will not be, "What knowledge is of the most worth?" but "What kinds of human beings do we wish to produce?" The possibilities virtually defy our imagination.[2]

What does Vice President Gore — whom George Will calls "the most radical person ever nominated by either major party" — have in mind when he calls for a "wrenching transformation of society" and a change of "the very foundation of our civilization"?[3]

If you wonder why Johnny can't read, Thomas Stict may give us a clue. Stict, a member of the U.S. Secretary of Labor's Commission on Achieving Necessary Skills, says, "Changing values is probably more important than reading."[4]

Harold Shane, Project Director of the NEA, weighs in with a strange statement:

> As young people mature, we must help them develop . . . a service ethic which will educate our young for planetary service and eventually for some form of world citizenship. . . . Implicit with the "global servant" concept are the moral insights that will help us live with the regulated freedom we must eventually impose upon ourselves.[5]

"Regulated freedom"? Figure that one out.

What does Theodore R. Sizer of the Coalition for Essential Schools mean when he says, "Sermonizing denies individual autonomy, which, with justice, lies at the heart of a new morality"?[6]

Benjamin Bloom, one of the fathers of Mastery Learning (OBE's prototype), sums up the philosophy of these apostles of apostasy: "The purpose of education is to change the thoughts, actions, and feelings of students."[7]

Now you know why author Samuel Blumenfeld calls the NEA "the Trojan Horse in American education,"[8] while *Forbes* magazine refers to it as the "National Extortion Association."[9]

Few will agree with everything in this book, but universal agreement was not a goal of the author. I would be surprised if my views are greeted with quiet acquiescence by all who read them. If you survive until the last chapter, your suggestions for turning things around may be better than mine. In which case, go for it!

I have striven for accuracy and tried to be fair, but I make no bones about my strong feelings. Here I have taken Pat Buchanan's advice: "Always err on the side of boldness."

When told that the whole world was against him, Martin Luther replied, "Then I am against the whole world."

I love everybody, and I'm a nice guy, but I have zero tolerance for the architects of the brave new world in whose hands the children are pawns.

Cicero long ago warned, "A nation can survive its fools, and even the ambitious. But it cannot survive treason from within."[10]

Now say a prayer and turn the page.

INTRODUCTION

The Betrayal

In the rooms of a Rancho Santa Fe mansion, 39 victims of mass suicide — wearing Nike shoes and black T-shirts — were discovered lying on their beds. The media spent days — even weeks — exploring every aspect of the bizarre event in California, analyzing the strange world of the cults, and ferreting out and imploring experts for answers.

At the same time, the Michigan doctor who has supervised the suicides of nearly 50 victims, went about his deadly business with barely a brief mention on the evening news. Dr. Jack Kevorkian, who has forgotten his Hippocratic oath and whose arrogance is exceeded only by that of his attorney's, seems to relish his role as "Dr. Death."

How did we get from Plymouth Rock and the Mayflower Company to Dr. Jack Kevorkian, who suggests,

"Ethics is saying and doing what is right at the time";[1] and the girl who called the talk show to say, "Old times and new morals don't mix"?

At what point did we exchange principle for expediency and the truth of God for the Lie?

SEARCHING FOR ANSWERS

After growing up in a small Midwestern town, I went away to college and university, and then invested 25 years in the pastorate in the Midwest and on the West coast.

When I first went to preach in New England several years ago, I was introduced firsthand to the America of our forefathers. As a result, questions arose in my mind concerning the old world: What happened to that world? How did the Puritans disappear from the pages of history and where did they go?

I pursued these questions with single-mindedness. Returning again and again to the scenes of our earliest history, I traveled the back roads, searching out old landmarks, weed-strewn cemeteries, and the historical churches. I pawed through old book stores and perused thousands of columns of print. I visited America's earliest institutions of higher learning.

Few Americans realize that Harvard University was founded in 1636 by a godly man and for one explicit purpose — the training of young men for the Christian ministry. Harvard, once dedicated to the gospel of Jesus Christ, is now a bastion of liberalism and recently welcomed Jane Fonda, who spoke of "the myth" of Christianity.

Harvard University was founded by a godly man for one explicit purpose — to train young men for Christian ministry.

On my visit to Yale University, I thought of Rev. Timothy Dwight who became president in 1795, at a time when the university bore little resemblance to the passion and purpose of its founders. Under Dwight's dynamic leadership a revival broke out that not only impacted Yale students but touched the entire country.

Who would have thought that the sons of such pioneers would come to regard God as a kind of pariah to be expunged from public life and erased from the moral consciousness? Who would have believed that a people whose fathers sacrificed so much to establish a nation under God would, in the 20th century, teach atheism in the schools and sex education without a moral base, approve of "partial birth abortion" — a nice name for infanticide — and discuss same-sex marriage in the halls of legislatures?

REASONS TO WEEP

Bearing His cross to the place of execution, Jesus was accompanied by His mother and other devoted women who loved Him. When Jesus saw them weeping, He turned and said, "Daughters of Jerusalem, do not weep for Me, but weep for yourselves and for your children" (Luke 23:28).

We have plenty of reasons to weep for ourselves and our children:

■ A million American kids run away from home each year!

■ A million and a quarter teenage girls get pregnant each year — that's one out of ten!

■ One out of five children are physically or sexually abused!

■ Kids spend more time watching TV than at school, church, or in significant family time combined!

■ Violent crimes committed by teenagers have doubled in the past 25 years!

■ One out of two marriages in the U. S. fails, and children of divorce are increasing by 1.1 million each year!

■ Of children born in 1989, one of three will be living on welfare sometime during their first 18 years!

■ At least half a million kids attempt suicide each year, and six thousand of them succeed — with many more killing themselves in violent accidents![2]

But what do statistics tell you?

In my travels across America, I meet people from every walk of life who are impacted by the social and moral decline in our nation.

Allow me to take a few entries from my diary.

A pastor in Washington state told me he had been asked to serve on a human resources committee at the local high school. One of his assignments was to read essays written by seniors. "Almost none of the upcoming graduates could compose a decent sentence or spell words accurately," he noted sadly.

People from every walk of life are impacted by the social and moral decline in our nation.

A grandmother I met requested prayer for her 13-year-old granddaughter: "She's been threatened by three girls if she doesn't join their gang."

A young man in his twenties told me, "I complained to my teachers that I couldn't read, but they told me not to worry. I finally quit school in the eleventh grade."

A pastor said, "I can't even let my 17-year-old daughter walk down to the 7-11 store at two o'clock in the afternoon!"

In one small town, a couple told me their 18-year-old son had been fatally stabbed a month earlier by a 13-year-old.

A midwestern teacher related the incident of a youngster who came to school with a manual on how to build terrorist weapons. "And another boy had graphic pornography," he told me. "Both students said the material was easily accessed on the Internet."

Is this the Internet the President wants every eighth grader logged onto? If you think it's difficult for a parent to monitor student textbooks, wait until they install computers in each classroom.

This same teacher was recently fired because he would not participate in a program that teaches homosexuality as an appropriate lifestyle.

While I was visiting in another church, a public school teacher told me of a boy she had disciplined for using the most obscene language in class. The school principal, however, reprimanded the teacher, saying that "swearing is part of the boy's culture."

That incident is relatively minor compared to a response from Washington D.C. school administrators. When fourth graders engaged in sexual activity in a classroom, the principal, without notifying the parents, dismissed the encounter because it was "consensual."[3]

AIM FOR THE CHILDREN

Something is dreadfully wrong when 40 percent of eight-year-olds can't read, and when — by the most conservative estimates — 23 million high school graduates are functionally illiterate.

Is there a solution? The government thinks so and proposes spending $2.7 billion for volunteers to tutor children, enabling students to read by the time they enter the fourth grade.

I have two questions: Why do we need $2.7 billion for "volunteers"? And what are the teachers teaching in the first, second, and third grades?

Could all this "dumbing down" have been by design?

In colonial America, children were reading at three and four years of age and were ready for college at 13 and 14. Now our stated goal is to teach kids how to read by the fourth grade and how to log onto the Internet by the eighth grade. By then students will be so "dumbed down," they will stare blankly at the screen and believe whatever they're told.

Could all this "dumbing down" have been by design? Renowned educator Thomas Sowell thinks so.

"Despite the economic prosperity of our country, the indicators of social degeneracy are all around us," Sowell writes. "The students' ignorance and inability to think, in even our best schools and colleges, mean that they are ripe prey for demagogues — with the future of this country correspondingly jeopardized."

Is there a deliberate attack on the minds and morals of our children? If so, it must be exposed and the trends reversed if we are to continue as a free people.

I believe — and will prove in the coming pages — that an attempt was begun long ago to change the direction of this country. The architects of that attempt were enemies of the gospel of Jesus Christ and diametrically opposed to the principles and values of the Founding Fathers.

The chosen method devised to alter our course called for the capture of the minds and souls of the children. Why? Because it would be too difficult to "improve" society through legislation.

"Men are cast-iron but children are wax."

Finding adults too resistant to change, these agents of change hit on a new idea: Aim for the children.

In 1837, Horace Mann, who would become the first secretary of education, wrote:

> Having found the present generation composed of materials almost unmalleable, I am about transferring my efforts to the next. Men are cast-iron but children are wax.[4]

Instead of trying to change those already set in their ways, America's educators set out to mold young minds still pliable and easily molded in the classroom.

THE BETRAYERS

TV Guide carried an ad for a cable system that boasted: "Guaranteed to break at least 20 percent more commandments than any other line-up."

It will take more than government regulations and V-chips to safeguard our homes from cheap sex and gratuitous violence — not to mention the mindless idiocy of the talk shows. Asking Hollywood to police itself is like asking the fox to guard the hen house.

William J. Bennett said, "If we ridicule and caricature traditional religious beliefs, standards of decency, and virtue . . . there will be a cost. It will be primarily to our children."[5]

Already the cost is too high. Already children are dying from unanswered questions.

A member of the rock band Luxury, referring to the star musician who took his own life, said, "Kurt Cobain looked for answers, and no answers were given. These unanswered questions are what killed him."

Already America's youth are the victims of a sinister, systematic betrayal.

Where is the assault taking place? Within the hollowed halls of America's classrooms, at the movie theaters, in front of our own television sets, through CD headsets. Anywhere God is not welcome an insidious and relentless barrage of immoral propaganda warps the minds of innocent children and ridicules the values that made our nation great.

Who perpetrates this betrayal?

■ A society immersed in self-fulfillment, consumed by materialism, lost in a fog of debt, and unaware of the forces shaping the lives of its children.

■ A church that has lost its passion for God and its sense of eternity. A church weakened by a steady secularization and reflecting the culture rather than impacting it.

■ An entertainment industry that long ago abandoned the most minimal standards of decency.

■ Educators more interested in salary, tenure, and political power than in teaching children to read and write.

■ A world system that deifies man and declares God to be irrelevant: "No deity will save us; we must save ourselves."

■ Hypocritical politicians who traffic in children's causes for personal gain. These cowardly "children's rights" activists mask their naked grab for political power behind starving faces and call for educational "reform."

When a young mother pushed her car into a lake, drowning her sons, all America was outraged by such cold-blooded betrayal. Many still weep for the dead youngsters.

Those same Americans, however, remain unmoved by the gradual corrosive influence of humanistic philosophy in music and television, education and religion. Why the silent acquiescence in the face of such a brazen assault on our children?

"NOT THIS BOY!"

Amram and Jochebed. Strange names, perhaps. You may not recognize them, but you know the name of their son, Moses — arguably the greatest man in the Old Testament — but a child born under sentence of death.

Fearful that the Hebrew slaves of the Nile were multiplying too fast and could soon mount a threat to his throne, Pharaoh ordered the deaths of every male child born to the hated clan.

When Moses was born, his parents took one look at that little wrinkled face and said, "Not this boy. He will not die. This is a child of destiny. He does not belong to the king or to the state; he does not belong to himself. He belongs to God!"

Moses did not die, but with the rod of God in his hand he changed the course of human history.

Once again the battle lines are drawn. The sentence of death has been pronounced on America's children. The conflict has been engaged.

It remains for us to trace the history of the conflict, to identify the participants, to acquaint ourselves with the issues, and — armed with truth — to rise to the defense of hearth and home.

If we fail to act, who will pay the price for our apathy? It probably won't be you or me. It will be America's children.

CHAPTER ONE

A Walk Down 16th Street

One warm sunny Saturday afternoon, I drove over the Potomac River and up 17th Street. After parking my car across from the Old Executive Office Building and around the corner from a favorite coffee shop, I took off on foot across Pennsylvania Avenue.

A day off between speaking engagements allowed time for a visit to our nation's capital.

When I set out to locate one of Washington's historic churches, I could not have known that I would find a cluster of buildings nearby, which — like pieces of a puzzle when fit together — illustrate the connection between unbelief in religion, compromise in public life, and corruption in government.

FOUNDRY UNITED METHODIST CHURCH

After crossing Lafayette Park, I asked a policeman for directions to Foundry United Methodist Church. I knew the Washington landmark to be somewhere on 16th Street.

For 180 years, presidents from Lincoln to Clinton have worshiped at this historic church. Although Bill Clinton is a Southern Baptist — who sang in the choir at Immanuel Baptist Church in Little Rock when he was governor of Arkansas — Hillary Clinton prefers the Methodist church. When they came to Washington, the Clintons settled on Foundry United Methodist.

John Wesley, founder of Methodism, once said,

I am not afraid that the people called Methodists should ever cease to exist either in Europe or America. But I am afraid lest they should exist only as a dead sect, having the form of religion without the power. And this undoubtedly will be the case unless they hold fast both the doctrine, spirit, and discipline with which they first went out.[1]

His worst fear realized, Wesley would have wept standing on the steps of this old church.

Foundry United Methodist has long since abandoned its commitment to a "literalistic" view of the Bible. In fact, the old-time "shouting Methodists" would find a lukewarm welcome here.

Its present pastor, Rev. J. Phillip Wogaman, "has warned that drug abuse, murder, unethical business practices, family breakups and homelessness have been created by 'unrestrained laissez-faire capitalism.'"[2]

He advocates the nationalization of oil companies and insists that a world government is the only solution to global conflict — a far cry from Wesley's injunction to his preachers: "You have nothing to do but to save souls. Therefore spend and be spent in this work."

United Methodist minister Harry Rieley recently declared, "Jesus is speaking as a gay man to the church today. The United Methodist Church has been supporting the persecution of human beings."

We shouldn't be surprised to learn, then, that a homosexuality symposium was recently held at Foundry Methodist.

Mark Tooley, Director of the Institute for Religion and Democracy, describes the event:

Keynote speaker, Episcopal Church in the USA Bishop John Spong, ridiculed the Christmas Nativity story, speculated about Jesus as a "drag queen," had praise for homosexual marriage and a declaration that the Ten Commandments are "immoral."

The daylong "celebration" at Foundry Church . . . surprised even the mostly homosexual audience of several hundred persons with their denial of religious beliefs.

"If a star led the Wise Men to the baby Jesus, then why couldn't King Herod find Him?" Bishop Spong asked a laughing audience. . . .

Noting that he has 15 "out-of-the-closet priests" in his own New Jersey diocese, Spong recalled with pride that the first woman he ordained in 1977 later declared her lesbianism. "I have given my all to this life and death struggle within the Episcopal Church," he declared. "I will sacrifice my career if I must."

Asked about the possibility of depicting Christ as a "drag queen," Wogaman responded, "I don't condemn it. I just don't know. I'll have to think about it some more." He pledged the Foundry Church would be "welcoming to the homosexual community."

. . . During the service, male couples held each other and kissed in the pews. One worship leader identified herself as a "lesbian Unitarian." A priest asked God "to help us to be true to ourselves."[3]

Such blasphemy occurred in a church that once had protracted meetings lasting for weeks.

GLORIOUS REVIVALS

Dwight L. Moody was invited to preach at Foundry Church, and Gypsy Smith held revivals that saw the altars lined with penitents.

The church historian writes:

The 1863 revival, a "glorious" one, continued for weeks with "encouraging results."

. . . Even in the midst of building a new church in 1864 and 1865, annual revivals were held. During the first of these, people had a "mind to work." Souls were converted each week. The pastor and the congregation worked "heartily together," and the church enjoyed a genuine revival. The second year, 1865, the revival continued for more than eight weeks. About 150 were convicted.

Another revival broke out at Foundry Methodist in 1878.

As it continued, "it increased in force." By September 19, all-day services were held. . . . The effect of it spread for miles. People began coming a distance of 30 miles to attend. . . . So great was the interest in it that most churches found it impossible to do more than maintain their regular services.

Fifty, one hundred, two hundred, two hundred and twenty-five conversions were reported in weekly accounts published in church periodicals. The *Washington Post* likened it to the great revival of 1857 and 1858 which swept the country. "There has been nothing like it in the history of those who are now members of this church." During the 40 days, over 550 people went to the altar.[4]

Abraham Lincoln was a Life Director of Foundry and contributed to the missions fund. Other presidents who worshiped there or attended on occasion were Andrew Johnson, Ulysses S. Grant, Rutherford B. Hayes, Harry Truman, and Franklin Roosevelt.[5]

How do you measure the influence of one church in the life of a city or a nation? At what point does compromise in the pulpit translate to havoc in the homes and disorder in the streets? It is certain that the ripple effect of apostasy in the house of God is staggering in its impact and long lasting in its duration.

At what point does compromise in the pulpit translate to havoc in the homes and disorder in the streets?

THE PASSING OF HELL

Although Foundry United Methodist is only one of 87 churches out of the denomination's 37,000 that rejects Methodism's disapproval of homosexual practices, the denomination is losing members nonetheless. In fact, in the past 20 years, two million Methodists have left — "the greatest loss in so short a period ever sustained by an American denomination," notes Robert E. Coleman.

"And though some leaders have expressed alarm and called for renewal," Mr. Coleman writes, "by and large the cancer of theological apostasy that eats at the vitals of evangelism is not being addressed."[6]

Such indifference is not peculiar to Methodism, however.

Martin Marty, church historian at the University of Chicago, has observed that "the passing of hell from modern consciousness is one of the major, if still undocumented, trends," of our time.

I can understand why. After all, who wants to hear about hell and the eternal consequence of sin when sensual, erotic pleasure has become your god? In this age of political and religious correctness, pastors and Sunday school teachers fear alienating their congregations and thus deny America's children the truth about hell.

For 125 years, every school child in America studied from that wonderful little volume, *The New England Primer.* Its best advertisement: "It taught millions to read, and not one to sin."

Religion was the core of the school curriculum, as the following reading indicates:

That I was brought to know
The danger I was in,
By nature and by practice too
A wretched slave of sin,

That I was led to see
I can do nothing well
And whither shall a sinner flee
To save himself from hell?

Today, hell is merely a casual swear word that for most children contains no hint of the horror of its eternal punishment — and, thus, no reason to try to avoid it.

Leaving the church, I walked back down 16th Street, musing on the impact of religion in American life and wondering, How long can the mainline denominations survive, having forsaken the absolute authority of Scripture and denying the power of the gospel? And how can a nation endure when its pulpits are no longer aflame with righteousness?

THE NEA WORM IN THE APPLE

I had gone only a block or two when I looked across the street and saw an impressive building with large gold letters set in marble — National Education Association — the formidable NEA.

From the church to the schoolhouse — this "schoolhouse," however, bears no resemblance to the small frame structures that once dotted the countryside and produced the best-educated people in the history of the world.

A recent *Forbes* magazine article described the NEA as "the worm in the American education apple."[7]
Why?

Syndicated columnist James Kilpatrick provides the answer: "The NEA in recent years has come to embody every single cause that has contributed to the crisis that threatens our public schools."[8]

In *The Family Under Siege,* George Grant traces the rise of the NEA organization that education pioneer Samuel Blumenfeld calls the "Trojan Horse in American education."

> Founded in 1857 by representatives of several state teachers associations, the National Education Association is today the country's largest labor union.
>
> For nearly 30 years, the union has maintained a smothering monopoly over every aspect of America's government-run educational system — from the content of the curriculum to the proposal of budgets, from the design of facilities to the administration of bureaucracies, from classroom methodology to teacher salaries, from political reform to regulatory control.[9]

What makes the NEA union "one of the most powerful forces in American life today"? Money and members.

- A membership of nearly three million.
- An annual combined budget of $500 million.
- A standing political war chest of nearly $20 million.

The NEA also has political, economic, and educational clout:

- The largest single interest group lobbying in Washington.
- The largest and richest political action committee.
- The biggest broker of group insurance benefits.
- The major ideological force in more than 90 percent of the nation's some 16,000 local public school districts.

Author and educator Phoebe Courtney notes that the union is not satisfied simply to control public education. "It wants complete control over all America's education — private as well as public," she writes. "It has vowed to bring private education under its control through teacher certification and state accreditation laws."[10]

Now let me get this straight. The NEA is a union of teachers, principals, and administrators working very hard to educate our children. They spend a lot of money, appoint committees, go to meetings, print brochures, formulate programs, lobby politicians, attend conferences, give speeches, set goals, and initiate reform.

The only problem is:

Johnny can't read and Susie can't spell. Willie can't write and Alice can't add. Teacher competency is down. Administrative effectiveness is down. Student advancement is down. Tests scores are down. Everything to do with our public school system is down — everything that is except crime, drug abuse, illicit sex, and the cost to the taxpayers.[11]

Although we spend more than any other industrialized nation on education, the results are meager.

The late Albert Shanker, president of the American Federation of Teachers, said, "Ninety-five percent of kids who go to college in the United States would not be admitted to college anywhere else in the world."[12]

A report from the National Commission of Excellence in Education makes this stinging indictment: "If an unfriendly foreign power had attempted to impose on America a mediocre educational system, it could not have devised one worse than the one we presently have."[13]

TEACHERS OR "CHANGE AGENTS"?

What's going on here? What's the purpose of that building across the street? What's the meaning of this collection and expenditure of funds, this ceaseless round of activities?

Scott Thompson, executive director of the National Association of Secondary School Principals, gives us a clue: "The NEA no longer contributes to the improvement of teaching and learning for students. It looks after the narrow interests of its members rather than after the broader interests of its constituency."[14]

The union itself admits as much:

> The major purpose of our association is not the education of children, it is or ought to be the extension and preservation of our members' rights. We earnestly care about the kids' learning, but that is secondary to the other goals.[15]

Educating children is not their major purpose? Aren't they an organization of teachers and educators?

Troubling thoughts, disquieting questions and concerns cloud my mind.

These are my children, my grandchildren. What right have the educational elite with their socio-political agendas to take our young people and brainwash them, heal them of the "insanity" derived from parents and churches, to "socialize" them and remake them to fit the shape of their brave new world?

President Clinton, in a recent speech, said: "When we start a new century, in a new millennium, in a completely new world, changing the way we work and live. . . ."

Wait a minute! What is this "completely new world"?

What's wrong with the old world? What's wrong with the way our fathers worked and lived? Why is everyone talking about "change"?

Teachers are now "change-agents." Is it a fetish?

I have no hankering after the one-room school-house with straight-back chairs and outdoor toilets. But neither am I prepared to surrender our children to the union bosses and power brokers who know better than parents what their kids shall be taught. Why surrender control to teachers who are more determined to create a world in their own image than to teach Johnny to read and Susie to spell?

John Schaar, a researcher in school change, declared, "The future is not someplace we are going to, but one we are creating. The paths are not found, but made. And the activity of making them changes both the maker and the destination."[16]

This generation has charted its own course, resulting in chaos in our schools and violence in our streets.

At one time in America the future *was* a place we were headed, and we sought to find it. Paths *were* to be found — not made — because somebody had put them there.

Today educators think we're far too advanced for that. Instead of acknowledging that Somebody has already delineated a path for mankind to follow, this generation has charted its own course and made its own way.

The result of this choice? Chaos in our schools and violence in our streets.

WHERE'S THE MORAL OUTRAGE?

Like clothes in a dryer, these disturbing thoughts tumbled around in my head as I continued down 16th Street.

Suddenly, I'm standing in front of an elegant building, my mind computing its name and retrieving its significance: the Jefferson Hotel. Isn't this the expensive hide-out of the political consultant who turned presidential politics on its ear?

When President Clinton seemed "irrelevant" after the 1994 Republican capture of Congress, it was Dick Morris who came to the rescue, crafting a strategy that single-handedly — according to Morris — resulted in Clinton's reelection.

Here in the Jefferson Hotel, Morris relaxed in a $440-a-night room. When it was disclosed that he was not alone in his comfy quarters, Dick Morris' stock fell like a shooting star. But not to worry. His fall was merely a prelude to better things.

Most Americans, inured to scandal, took the ugly disclosure in stride. It seems nothing bothers us much anymore.

"We've lost our capacity for shame," a *Time* reporter said on CNN's "Talk Back Live."

"Where's our moral outrage?" asked columnist Linda Chavez. "The Spanish have a phrase for it: *sin verguenza.* It means without shame, and it's no compliment."

Chavez went on to say,

> It could become the motto of our age, exemplified most recently by Dick Morris, the President's strategist who resigned after a tabloid published pictures of him at a hotel with a prostitute. Instead of retreating from the media spotlight when his antics with a $200-a-night call girl became public, Morris is actually looking for new ways to expose himself.[17]

Chavez then quoted Sen. Daniel Patrick Moynihan, D-N.Y., who wrote a brilliant essay in *The Public Interest*. He described the social deterioration occurring from out-of-wedlock births to skyrocketing crime. "Much of the problem stemmed," he said, "from a phenomenon he dubbed 'defining deviancy down.'"

"In other words," Ms. Chavez noted, "so lowering our standards about what is proper that what once would have been considered deviant behavior has become merely individual choice. In fact, the situation is worse than Moynihan described. We've not only done away with concepts of right and wrong, but we've also begun to heap huge rewards on those whose actions would once have made them pariahs. Why should Dick Morris be ashamed of himself when so many of us are eager to shower him with fame and fortune?"[18]

In commenting on the Jefferson Hotel scandal, the *Chicago Tribune* weighed in with a piece titled, "Shame, Shame: Trading on Infamy":

In the unlikely event you were inclined to, don't bother shedding any tears for Dick Morris. The future looks bright for President Clinton's former political advisor — at least the financial future. He lost his job. . . . What a break! Morris is disgraced as a political advisor, but he has made it onto the celebrity gravy train. Celebrity can be minted either from fame or from infamy; what counts is cashing in on it. . . . Shame seems to be fighting an uphill battle.[19]

Morris is back and richer than ever. His fall from grace paved the way for a million dollar book deal, public appearances, and network assignments. And life goes on.

PLANNED PARENTHOOD'S WILLING PARTNER

My stroll down 16th Street has been an eye-opener, but it's not over. In the next block stands yet another link in the chain that shackles this generation: the Washington headquarters of Planned Parenthood of America.

Here at PP the daughters of Margaret Sanger labor night and day to alter the behavior of our kids. Under the guise of "compassion" and "enlightened" social progress, they contribute to a nightmare for millions of youngsters — a nightmare underwritten with your tax dollars.

Your 13-year-old daughter may need parental approval to have her ears pierced and permission from home to receive an aspirin at school, but an abortion is provided under a cloak of secrecy. Mother will never know.

But God will know, and a baby will die — and a 13-year-old girl will cry in the night and go to her grave bearing scars inflicted by adults who should have been her protectors but who became her exploiters.

What is Planned Parenthood? George Grant answers that question in *The Family Under Siege:*

Planned Parenthood is the world's oldest, largest, and best organized provider of abortion and birth control services. From its humble beginnings around the turn of the century, when the entire shoestring operation consisted of a two-room, makeshift clinic in a run-down Brooklyn neighborhood staffed by three untrained volunteers, it has expanded dramatically into a multi-billion-dollar international conglomerate with programs and activities in 134 nations on every continent.[20]

Let's examine the statistics that George Grant provides about this massive organization. In the United States alone, Planned Parenthood:

■ Employs more than 20,000 staff personnel and volunteers.

■ Operates 922 clinics and 167 affiliates in every major metropolitan area, coast to coast.

■ Showed $23.5 million in 1992 earnings with $192.9 million in cash reserves and another $108.2 million in capital assets.

■ Has an estimated combined annual budget of more that a trillion dollars.

According to Grant, "Planned Parenthood may well be the largest and most profitable nonprofit organization in history."

In recent years, Planned Parenthood has found a willing partner in Bill Clinton. George Grant lists a string of strategic victories won by Planned Parenthood's association with the Clinton Administration:

■ Reestablished federally funded family planning clinics as abortion referral agencies.

■ Reinstated funding for abortion providers overseas through the Agency for International Development and other foreign aid bureaucracies.

■ Converted all overseas military hospitals into abortion facilities.

■ Won the right to undertake fetal research on aborted babies.

■ Lifted the Food and Drug Administration's importation and testing ban on the French abortifacient drug, RU 486.

■ Secured new tax funding from the American taxpayer for the United Nations Fund for Population Activity's brutal forced-abortion, infanticide, and sterilization program in China and India.

■ Reestablished tax funding of abortions in the District of Columbia.[21]

What motivates an entire organization of people — some of them medical professionals — to set out on a "seek and destroy" mission on innocent, pre-born babies?

To answer that question, I had to dig deeper.

"NO GODS! NO MASTERS!"

The Founder of Planned Parenthood, Margaret Sanger, was born in 1879, in Corning, New York. Life was not easy for the family of eleven children. Margaret's mother, although devoted to her husband and children, was never well.

Margaret, who described her childhood as "joyless and filled with drudgery and fear," could not wait to leave home. Almost immediately she plunged into a life of restless rebellion — a characteristic possibly gained from her father, Michael Higgins, who was something of a free thinker and skeptic.

The young woman dabbled in the fashionable progressivism of the day: radical politics, suffragette feminism, and promiscuous sex. After attending college for less than a year, Margaret dropped out and took a job as a kindergarten teacher for a while. Next she studied nursing but never finished the introductory course.

About that time she met and married William Sanger, a successful young architect. They moved to an upscale Manhattan apartment and soon had three children. But marriage, family, and housekeeping didn't satisfy the restlessness.

Margaret dabbled in politics, "attended rallies, meetings, and caucuses, and became acquainted with the foremost radicals of the day. . . . She joined the Socialist Party . . . and even helped agitate several strikes and labor protests."[22]

While attending rallies in Greenwich Village, she was exposed to "free love," which was openly discussed and practiced.

"No one championed sexual freedom as openly and ardently as Margaret. When she spoke, the others became transfixed."

She published a paper called *The Woman Rebel,* with the slogan, "No Gods! No Masters!" splashed across the masthead. In the eight-page pulp sheet she referred to marriage as a "degenerate institution," and sexual modesty as "obscene prudery."

She wrote that "rebel women claim the following rights: the right to be lazy, the right to be an unmarried mother, the right to destroy . . . and the right to love."[23]

This is the woman — obsessed with sex, "ardent propagandist for the joys of the flesh," proponent of free love, and opponent of every decent instinct in human life — who gave us Planned Parenthood — the organization that now teaches sex education in our schools.

What are the results of Sanger's crusade? Today more than 75 percent of America's districts teach sex education, and there are over 300 school-based "clinics" in operation. Yet the percentage of illegitimate births has only increased, "from a mere 15 percent to an astonishing 51 percent."[24]

To understand the true purpose behind Planned Parenthood's desire to offer birth control to women, consider this statement made by a former affiliate and abortion provider:

> Abortion is a skillfully marketed product sold to frightened young women at a crisis time of her life. As abortion providers, we knew that any time we went into a school, the pregnancy rate was going to go up by 50 percent.
>
> We knew we could sell abortions to every single classroom, but we couldn't just go in and say, "Look, our goal is actually for you to have three to five abortions between the ages of 13 and 18." No, no, we couldn't do that. So we said, "You know these kids need to abstain, and we know that, but they're not going to abstain, so we must teach them how to have safe sex."
>
> In the fifth and sixth grades, I came in. Now (after the gradual preparation in the earlier

grades) my agenda was clear: Get them to laugh at their parents and get them sexually active — get them on a method of birth control.

We would deliberately prescribe a low-dose birth control pill with a high rate of pregnancy. Don't miss what I just said. We prescribed a birth control pill we knew they would get pregnant on. (It had to be taken at the exact same time every day.)

Sexual activity goes up. And now she's pregnant. Who's she going to call? Me! Because I gave her a card that says, "Free pregnancy test. Licensed counselors. Telephone answered 24 hours a day." She calls that number, not understanding we just sell one product — abortion. Our people are skillfully trained to overcome every objection.[25]

Margaret Sanger would be pleased to know that the organization she founded is committed to the policies, programs, and priorities she espoused.

"We are merely walking down the path Mrs. Sanger carved out for us," asserted Dr. Alan Guttmacher, who succeeded her as president.

With its taxpayer funded treasury, nonprofit status, and school-based clinics, Planned Parenthood continues to play its part in the fraying of the fabric of American life.

At what point will we awaken from our long slumber to survey the damage done by the mind polluters and soul destroyers, operating under cover of government-sanctioned respectability? When will we begin the reconstruction required if we are to provide a decent environment for the next generation?

The dismantling of Planned Parenthood would be a good starting place.

We knew that any time we went into a school, the pregnancy rate was going to go up by 50 percent.
— Former abortion provider

A PRESIDENT MADE IN OUR IMAGE?

By now I've reached the corner of 16th and Hays Streets on the northwest side of Lafayette Park.

Across Pennsylvania Avenue, the White House sits barricaded behind a heavy iron fence. Since the bombings of the World Trade Center and the Federal Building in Oklahoma City, concrete barriers have closed the avenue to all but pedestrian traffic.

But are fences tall enough or barriers strong enough to keep us safe when we cannot agree on what is evil? Now instead of fighting evil as a unified force, Americans focus on debating whether evil even exists. Character no longer matters to a people who have forgotten that sin is a disgrace to a nation.

When the people of God in the Old Testament desired a king, God granted their request and gave them Saul — an outwardly impressive man, tall and strong with an engaging personality.

An unredeemed character flaw, however, was the undoing of the poor king. Defeated in battle and rejected by the Lord, Saul passed by the witch of Endor on his way to the grave. The reign that began with an anointing ended with the occultic by the king who mirrored the people.

"This was the leader *they* wanted," I heard one preacher say. "Before the people got Saul, they *became* Saul."

In Robert H. Bork's *Slouching Towards Gomorrah,* the distinguished conservative scholar offers a troubling view of a culture in decline. Of our own President, Bork writes:

Thirty years ago, Clinton's behavior would have been absolutely disqualifying. Since the 1992 election, the public has learned far more about what is known, euphemistically, as the "character issue." Yet none of this appears to affect Clinton's popularity. It is difficult not to conclude that something about our moral perceptions and reactions has changed profoundly. If that change is permanent, the implication for our future is bleak.[26]

Maureen Down, writing in the *New York Times,* puts the character issue in perspective:

It is futile to argue that Mr. Clinton is flawed because all he does is respond and change. That's exactly why people like him. We are in a consumer culture. Baby boomers are the most spoiled, over-marketed cohort in history, accustomed to having products tailored to them. Why should the presidency be any different?

The joke is, we're looking to Bill Clinton for continuity and stability, and he's looking to us for continuity and stability. But even if we don't like what we see in the mirror, we can't blame the President. The image is our own.[27]

No one has a franchise on evil, nor is corruption confined to one political party. There's enough sinning to go around. After all, the devil is an equal opportunity employer.

ON A FREE FALL

The times cry out for a prophet. Isaiah would take one look at the barren wasteland of our times, with its disappearing chunks of morality, and cry:

Alas, sinful nation, a people laden with iniquity, a brood of evildoers, children who are corrupters! They have forsaken the Lord, they have provoked to anger the Holy One of Israel, they have turned away backward (Isaiah 1:4).

Twenty-five hundred years ago, Jeremiah watched with horror as his nation, careless and headstrong, plummeted to judgment. Rejecting discipline, scoffing at warnings, and despising the messenger who delivered them, they went on their way.

At some point they crossed the line. When the people committed an indelible sin, the prophet delivered the stinging indictment: "The sin of Judah is written with a pen of iron; with the point of a diamond it is engraved on the tablet of their heart" (Jeremiah 17:1).

Nothing could stop the free fall — nothing but judgment.

I wonder what Jeremiah would have thought had he walked with me down 16th Street that Saturday afternoon.

I think he would have wept as he lamented: "An astonishing and horrible thing has been committed in the land: The prophets prophesy falsely, and the priests rule by their own power; and My people love to have it so. But what will you do in the end?" (Jeremiah 5:30,31).

Could we — or our children and grandchildren — be asking that same question someday?

CHAPTER TWO

The Decade of Decision

To understand the moral quagmire of the last days of this century, we must revisit "the decade that changed America" — the 1960s.

"The stones we threw into the waters of our world in those days," Peter Collier has written, "caused ripples that continue to lap on our shores today — for better, and more often, for worse."[1]

Cal Thomas agrees: "If you slept through the Sixties you woke to a different America. It was the pivotal point of the past — an authentic decade of decision."[2]

Has any culture in history ever discarded its belief system as quickly as America did during that period? The rapidity with which we exchanged objective truth for a variety of subjective myths is both astonishing and frightening.

Syndicated columnist David Broder warns, "The facts of social disintegration are so staggering, this is no longer a matter of ideological argument. . . . it is no longer possible to pretend that the values by which people live their lives don't matter."[3]

Something happened a generation ago that threw our world out of kilter and touched every facet of life in America.

Has any culture ever discarded its belief system as quickly as America did during the 1960s?

The generation gap left families fractured and bewildered. Parents lost control of their children. Big government with bloated bureaucracies intruded on family life and private business. At the same time, courts struck down freedoms that had stood since brave men mutually pledged to each other their lives, their fortunes, and their sacred honor.

In 1787, 55 delegates gathered in Philadelphia to write a document that would define the future and secure the freedoms of our young republic. From 13 colonies they came, possessed of a love of country, passionate patriotism, and a strong commitment to liberty.

One hundred and seventy-six years later, another group met in another place to draft a document for a different purpose. Motivated by love for nothing but themselves, they were driven by hate — hate for the nation and contempt for its people.

Robert J. Bork, in his book, *Slouching Towards Gomorrah*, narrates this defining moment in American history:

> The Sixties were born at a particular time and place: June, 1962, the AFL-CIO camp at Port Huron, Michigan. Though most Americans have never heard of the proceedings at Port Huron, they were crucial for the authentic spirit of Sixties' radicalism issued there. That spirit spread and evolved afterwards, but its later malignant stages, including violence, were implicit in its birth.[4]

Bork describes the participants as "an early convention of SDS (Students for a Democratic Society)." At that point they were "a small group of alienated, left-wing college students . . . 59 delegates from 11 campus chapters."

Their creed? "Four square against anti-Communism, eight-square against American culture, twelve-square against sell-out unions, one-hundred-twenty square against an interpretation of the Cold War that saw it as a Soviet plot and identified American policy fondly."

"In short they rejected America," Bork writes. "Worse, as their statement of principles made clear, they were also four-square against the nature of human beings and features of the world that are unchangeable."

DAWN OF A NEW AGE?

Judge Bork describes the Port Huron Statement drafted by Tom Hayden as "a lengthy, stupefyingly dull manifesto with ignorance and arrogance proper to adolescents."

"We regard men as infinitely precious and possessed of unfulfilled capacities for reason, freedom, and love," SDS proclaimed. The phrase, "unfulfilled capacities" was substituted for the statement in Hayden's draft that man was "infinitely perfectible."

Bork explains that Hayden's original words "express the view common to totalitarian movements, that human nature is infinitely malleable so that a new, better, and perhaps perfect nature can be produced by the rearrangement of social institutions. Since actual humans resist attempts to remake their natures, coercion and, ultimately, violence will be required. The initial rhetoric of the movement, however, before disillusion set in, was one of peaceful aspiration."

The Port Huron Statement continued, "Human brotherhood must be willed as a condition of future survival and as the most appropriate form of social relations."

"But to talk of brotherhood," Bork writes, "to exalt man's ability to create a world free of war and want, where reason, freedom and love replace inequality and discrimination is dangerously unrealistic."

They planned to do this, of course, without the help of a supernatural Being.

What was the SDS proposing? To use politics "to bring their secular vision of the kingdom of God to fruition on earth, now," Bork explains. It is "an ideal that the most devout and active Christians have never remotely approximated for any community larger that a monastery, and probably not in any monastery."[5]

A small group of alienated college students gave birth to a new era of radicalism.

America was corrupt from top to bottom, and the Port Huron Statement sounded the alarm. It was a call to battle. These brave young soldiers would overturn the old order and trample on outmoded concepts like respect, reverence, order — even God.

"It felt like the dawn of a new age," one of the SDS delegates said. "It was exalting. . . . We thought we knew what had to be done, and that we were going to do it."[6]

Now, a generation later, Tom Hayden and the warriors of Grants Park have bathed, donned three-piece suits, and run for Congress. The radicals of the

1960s have melted into the establishment of the 1990s, but the damage is done. The wreckage is everywhere.

REDEFINING GOD AND FAMILY

In 1960, the family was still intact. There was little disagreement over its definition: Husband and wife, with or without children. Today confusion reigns over the meaning of the "traditional" family.

Radical feminist Betty Friedan claims families aren't dying or deteriorating, simply changing. She's quite explicit in her view that "we ought to get over our nostalgia for two-parent families headed by bread winner husbands and deal with the reality of family in all its variety."[7]

That reminds me of former surgeon general Jocelyn Elders who said we ought to "get over our love affair with the fetus."

The recent United Nations Fourth World Conference of Women in Beijing, China, was designed to undermine the family and to ridicule the role of the nurturing mother.

One feminist writer said, "Although many people think that men and women are the natural expression of a genetic blueprint, gender is a product of human thought and culture, a social construction that creates the 'true nature' of all individuals."[8]

In other words, biological differences between men and women are relatively insignificant, external features. This kind of thinking runs counter to everything taught in the Word of God.

The Bible says, "So God created man in His own image; in the image of God He created him; male and female He created them."[9]

If the family fared poorly in the Sixties, God didn't do so well either. The decade witnessed the most serious assault on religious freedom in our history. The Bible was thrown out of the schools, prayer became suspect in public places, and we witnessed the rise of militant secularism.

When public officials in Washington, D.C. called for a day of prayer, an ACLU spokesman said, "It is always inappropriate for government officials to ask citizens to pray."[10]

Such a statement betrays mind-boggling ignorance of every page of American history. Before the 1960s, the idea that America was a Christian nation went virtually unchallenged. Before we knew what hit us, however, a blind rage against Christ and religion obscured the most salient facts of our tradition.

One of the Chicago Seven — militant atheist Abbie Hoffman — proclaimed, "God is dead, and we did it for the kids."

Jim Morrison, lead singer for the Doors, spoke for many when he said, "I have always been attracted to ideas that were about revolt, disorder, chaos — especially activity that seems to have no meaning. It seems to me to be the road to freedom."[11]

In 1960, a stigma was attached to out-of-wedlock activity. I remember when a Hollywood star became pregnant by an Italian movie producer. The actress couldn't get a bit part in Hollywood for 20 years and eventually moved overseas.

Today, an actress or any female public figure could have a baby outside marriage — the father being her veterinarian, hair dresser, garbage man, or bill collector. It's almost a badge of honor, and she becomes a role model to millions of young girls.

The society that laments the epidemic of teenage pregnancy is the same society that encourages promiscuous sexual activity. The hypocrisy is breathtaking, the cost in human terms astronomical.

And heaven weeps.

**We lament the epidemic of
teenage pregnancy and at same time
encourage promiscuous sexual activity.**

PICKING AND CHOOSING

Herbert London, Professor of Humanities at New York University, was asked to serve as a TV commentator for a group of adolescents discussing "teenage morality."

One young lady noted, "I pick and choose what I believe is right. My parents told me I am the best judge of what is moral."

During the program, the teens could not agree that any behavior is wrong — except maybe murder but not much else.

"Is it any wonder," London asks, "that we cannot deal with the moral chaos that surrounds us? The muscle of moral behavior has atrophied from disuse as many people — not only teenagers — pick and choose their preferred morality."[12]

Patriotism has also taken a hit in the culture wars. Thirty-five years ago, I doubt that any classroom in America began without the Pledge of Allegiance. Today the Supreme Court of the United States has designated the burning of the American flag a form of free speech.

The father of a five-year-old told me he went to kindergarten and was shocked when the class stood and pledged allegiance "to the Universe and to all the creatures within."

Professor London expresses an appropriate concern when he writes:

I yearn for a time when family values and personal responsibility didn't have to be defined; when barbarism was routinely shunned. Those days may not return, but we would be wise to retrace our steps asking what went wrong and how can we recapture the moral and civic virtues of a less tortured era.[13]

Retracing our steps may not be pleasant. They will lead through the needle-strewn jungle of Haight-Ashbury, where flower children turned on and tuned out; the muddy fields of Woodstock, where young people, mesmerized by raucous music, sought for love in all the wrong places; and the Ivy League campuses, where brave university presidents surrendered to student activists who demonstrated their passion for peace by "occupying buildings, bringing firearms on campus, destroying manuscripts of books, assaulting and kidnapping officials, and murdering at least one student."[14]

Intoxicated by a sense of their own moral purity and superiority, they might well have remembered the words of Edmund Burke:

> Men are qualified for civil liberty in exact proportion to their disposition to put moral chains upon their own appetites. Society cannot exist unless a controlling power upon will and appetite be placed somewhere, and the less of it there is within, the more there is without. It is ordained in the eternal constitution of things that men of intemperate minds cannot be free.[15]

It is essential to understand that the rebellion leading to the chaos in the 1960s has changed its cloak but not its character in the 1990s. Its unrestrained impulse to evil — differing in style but not in substance — has ripped the fabric of our culture. The damage may be repaired, but only if the effort is immediate and sustained.

THE GROWING GAPING HOLE

Alan Bloom put his finger on the problem when he wrote in *The Closing of the American Mind*, "There is one thing a professor can be absolutely certain of. Almost every student entering the university believes, or says he believes, that truth is relative."[16]

When absolute truth — the only kind of truth there is — disappears, a fissure appears in the foundation of the moral order. As the gaping hole grows larger and larger, it eventually swallows up every pillar upon which a stable society rests.

What, then, is left? High schools that look more like prisons than prisons do; colleges and universities that devalue truth and jettison anything that is distasteful; and a student body ignorant of the price their forefathers paid for the very lecture halls they occupy.

I recall a debate at the Yale Political Union. When one young debater made a disparaging reference to "capitalism and the free enterprise system," the student audience erupted in thunderous applause.

I couldn't help but think: How hypocritical since most of these pampered law students are probably here because some capitalistic entrepreneurs — namely mom and dad — worked 18 hours a day to send their kids to college.

Another thought crossed my mind. If these students are so opposed to capitalism, why are they studying to be lawyers?

MYTH AS HISTORY

Anyone who has succeeded in any area of life realizes that achievement fosters self-esteem. Modern educators, however, see it the other way around.

In his book, *Slouching Towards Gomorrah*, Robert Bork notes that "a great deal of time is wasted at all levels of our educational system trying to build students' self-esteem, time that might better be spent teaching them skills and knowledge that would justify self-esteem."

Bork illustrates how colleges use the "self-esteem" issue to promote programs dedicated to women and to ethnic groups at the expense of truth and historical fact. Allow me to paraphrase an incident he records to illustrate this point.

A prominent Afrocentrist lecturing at Wellesley College stated that Greek civilization was stolen from Egypt and that Egyptians were black. He claimed, among other things, that Aristotle stole his famous philosophy from the library at Alexandria.

During the question period, a female professor asked the lecturer, "Why do you make that claim when the library at Alexandria was built after Aristotle's death?"

"I resent the tone of that question," was the Afrocentrist's only reply.

Afterwards, several students accused the female professor of racism. To make matters worse, her colleagues — who knew that the lecturer was making "historical misrepresentations" (lies) — did not support her objections.

When the female professor complained about the inaccuracies to the dean of the college and related what the Afrocentrist was teaching Wellesley students, the dean replied, "Each person has a different but equal view of history."

Why are academics afraid to challenge the misrepresentations of feminists and Afrocentrists? For fear of being labeled "sexist and racist."

As a result, "Black students are . . . taught myth as history," Bork points out and then notes the devastating consequences:

> The programs tend to be indoctrination rather than education. The presence of Afrocentrism on campus, like the presence of feminism, lowers scholarly standards generally. Professors outside the program refuse to object and refuse to demand evidence and logic when impossible claims are made.[17]

Truth is irrelevant when society can lie with a straight face as long as that lie advances the "cause" — whatever that cause may be. Isn't that how Hitler built his Nazi regime? On lies?

That brings to mind a memorable statement made by Washington D.C. mayor Marion Barry, "There are two kinds of truth, real truth and made-up truth."

In that kind of world, former senior advisor to President Clinton, George Stephanopulous, makes sense when he says, "We kept the promises we meant to keep."

Truth is irrelevant when society can lie with a straight face as long as that lie advances the "cause" — whatever that cause may be.

"WESTERN CULTURE'S GOTTA GO"

The deception of historical truth continues when sensible curriculum is substituted for feel-good subjects that merely encourage students in their adolescent rebellion against authority.

A case in point is Stanford's cowardly capitulation to a mindless minority who objected to a popular course on Western culture. Bork recounts the shameful incident:

> The university had a very popular required course in Western culture. The idea was that students should have at least a nodding acquaintance with the minds and works that have shaped the West and that constitute our heritage.
>
> But radicals and minorities objected both because Western culture should not be celebrated, being racist, sexist, violent, imperialistic, and not at all like those wonderful Third World

cultures, and because the authors that were assigned — Aristotle, Machiavelli, Rousseau, Locke, and Shakespeare — were all white males.

The culmination of the campaigning consisted of a conga line snaking across campus, led by Jesse Jackson, the protesters chanting, "Hey, hey, ho, ho, Western Culture's gotta go." And go it did.[18]

What happened? Stanford revised the course. The white male authors were replaced by women and writers "of color" who were bitterly hostile to Western civilization.

Judge Bork calls this kind of capitulation "a quota system for the curriculum."

The incident at Stanford makes it easy to understand why George Roche, president of Hillsdale College, said, "One of the best-kept secrets in American higher education today is that many colleges and universities are teetering on the brink of disaster."[19]

Allowing students to run the show, to choose the curriculum, to intimidate teachers and administrators — and even shut down the place if the mood hits them — makes as little sense as permitting passengers to fly the airplane.

When I fly, I want competence and authority in the cockpit, and we ought to have competent adult professionals in the classroom — professionals who

possess some convictions, who exhibit some character, and who have a commitment to time-honored
truths, as well as the skills to pass them on.

WHEN HIGHER LEARNING LOWERS ITS STANDARDS

Our colleges and universities have become clinics
where students are treated as if they were animals in
a research lab. Like guinea pigs they have become
objects for experimentation.

And what do parents — and students — receive in
return for the thousands of dollars spent on higher
education? Instead of an instruction that will prepare
them for a future career, they are exposed to courses
in meaningless trivia that makes a mockery of higher
learning.

In his book, *The Fall of the Ivory Tower,* George
Roche provides a sampling of courses offered at some
of America's major universities:

■ At Pennsylvania State University, it was possible
to earn a Leisure Studies degree in Golf Management.
Students christened it a "fore-year degree."

■ At Michigan State University, one could earn a
master's degree in "packaging."

■ The University of Pennsylvania granted a Ph.D.
for a dissertation on the New England clambake, and
the State University of New York granted one for
"Women's Shopping: A Sociological Approach."

■ At Stanford University, an upper division course
was called "Black Hair as Culture and History."

- Middlebury College in Vermont had a class devoted to the "eroticism, esthetics, voyeurism, and misogyny" of the films of Brigitte Bardot.
- Kent State offered "Camp Leadership," "Socio-Psychological Aspects of Clothing," "Basic Roller Skating," and "Dance Roller Skating."
- The University of Illinois offered "Pocket Billiards" and "The Anthropology of Play."
- Rutgers University devoted a course for German majors to "The Seduced Maiden Motif in German Literature."
- At Johns Hopkins University a course on biomedical research was taught using the format of "The Tonight Show."[20]

In the late 1980s — and still today, I suspect — it was possible, according to George Roche, to graduate from:

- 78 percent of the nation's colleges and universities without taking a course in the history of Western Civilization.
- 38 percent without taking any history course.
- 45 percent without taking an American or English literature course.
- 77 percent without taking a foreign language course.
- 41 percent without taking a mathematics course.
- 33 percent without studying the natural or physical sciences.[21]

Are there consequences to such sub-standard educational requirements?

Yes, according to a 1993 Rand Corporation study.[22] The report showed that over one-half of a national sample of college upper-class students were unable to perform cognitive tasks at a high school level.

A recent survey that polled American college faculty members about their students' performance found these startling results:

■ Three-quarters of the college faculty surveyed felt that their students did not meet preparation standards.

■ Only 15 percent of college faculty members say that their students are adequately prepared in mathematics and quantitative reasoning. (Higher-education faculty in Hong Kong, Korea, Sweden, Russia, Mexico, Japan, Chile, Israel, or Australia rated their incoming college students much higher.)

■ Only one in five American faculty members thinks students have adequate writing and speaking skills.[23]

Such results should not be surprising in light of the fact that, in 1988, only three percent of American high school seniors could describe their own television viewing habits in writing above an "adequate" level. In fact, the writing ability of American students is little short of appalling. American schools, according to the NAEP, produce few students who can write well.

Other skills are also lacking. In one college geography class, 25 percent of the students could not locate the Soviet Union on a world map, while on a map of the 48 contiguous states, only 22 percent of the class could identify 40 or more states correctly.

So if they aren't learning geography, what are college students studying?

GAY AND LESBIAN STUDIES

The book, *Comedy and Tragedy: College Course Descriptions and What They tell Us About Higher Education Today*, published by Young Americans Foundation, gives us a glimpse into the mindset of college professors:

> This fall the class of 2000 will embark on a four year journey at colleges and universities across the country from course offerings ranging from the bizarre (Harvard University's "Fetishism") to those having more to do with activism than scholarship (Cornell University's "Housing and Feeding the Homeless").[24]

Students may be left wondering what practical value can be derived from a 1990s college education. Parents, taxpayers, and alumni should also be concerned. Billions of dollars annually flow from their pockets into the coffers of academic institutions. All too often, this money is used to promote ideological pursuits rather than education.

Themes that form the core ideology of multiculturalism — race, class, gender, and sexual orientation — are no longer scattered through the curriculum but are now a dominant part of it. The prevalence of such themes does not substantially differ from one school to another. Students are forced to face the regime of political correctness at nearly every institution of higher learning.

Let's look at some of the courses on sex offered in colleges and universities. The fastest growing fields in all of academia is "gay and lesbian studies," with programs at 46 colleges and many others schools offering courses on the subject.

Here is a sampling of the courses offered:

- Brown University — "Daughters of Darkness: Lesbian Tropes"; "English 116A: Unnatural Acts"
- Cornell University — "Lesbian Personae"; "Gay Fiction"
- Dartmouth College — "Introduction to Gay and Lesbian Studies"; "Gay Male Literature"
- Duke University — "Gay Abandon"
- Amhearst College — "Representing Sexuality: Whitman to AIDS"; "The Cross Cultural Construction of Gender"
- Vasser College — "From Bohemia to Queer: Contemporary Lesbian and Gay Communities in America"

■ Georgetown University — "Unspeakable Lives: Gay and Lesbian Narratives"[25]

Remember, your tax dollars are helping to fund these courses in sodomy and perversion.

STUDENTS IN THE WAR ZONE

For many years, I have traveled almost weekly from one section of this country to the other. University and college students across the nation tell me they are ridiculed by professors for their moral standards.

The instructors challenge them: "Give it sixty days," they laugh, "and you'll have a completely different viewpoint of morality."

Students don't stand a chance anymore. Practical atheism is taught in our colleges and universities, premarital sex is routinely promoted, and abstinence is mocked or made to appear hopelessly out of date.

Someone suggested we send our young people into the universities and colleges as missionaries. "Let them bring a Christian testimony into the classroom," they say.

Forget it! To entrust your young people to teachers who have become "facilitators" and "change agents" — who ignore the Bible, hate Christ, and despise the country that provides more freedom and better opportunities than any people has ever known — is homicidal.

One history professor at the University of Massachusetts-Amherst begins the first day of class by announcing, "This class will be consistently un-American."

To send young people into that kind of environment makes as much sense as sending sixth graders to fight a war with sticks and stones against opponents three times their age and armed with hand grenades and bayonets.

We ought to be concerned about our testimony, and nothing is more important than winning souls to Jesus Christ. But if our witness is to be effective, the world must see the Christian family as a well-adjusted, disciplined, productive, law-abiding model for society.

Let others see in us a lifestyle that makes some sense in a world gone mad. If we don't, the decades to come will hinge less on "decision" and more on disaster.

CHAPTER THREE

Barbarians in the City

Americans have never flinched in the face of brute force. Twice in this century, the United States has fought in world wars to defend our freedoms and to liberate others. It remains to be seen if we retain the will to engage in the kind of conflict required to be victorious in the struggle for the very soul of our nation.

In the first decade of the fifth Christian century, wild Germanic tribes spilled over the hills in the north and swept over the fruitful vineyards and fertile fields of Italy, raping and pillaging as they moved toward its capital city. By the end of AD 410, Rome, the city of the Caesars, lay in ruins, sacked by the barbarians.

Today the Soviet Empire no longer exists, communism has been defeated, and the threat of nuclear holocaust has faded — at least, that is what we're led to believe. It is known, but seldom reported, that nuclear missiles could be retargeted in our direction — not in months or weeks or days — but in hours. In addition, the threat of madmen in North Korea, fanatics in Iran and Iraq, and the growing military machine of China are yet to be reckoned with.

Potential military conflict, however, is not America's greatest threat. Today our nation's enemies occupy government offices, publish our newspapers, control network television, produce Hollywood's movies, and dominate our public school systems.

If an external force were doing to America what we are doing to ourselves, we would be armed to the teeth, marching in the streets, demanding of our leaders a forceful response.

Potential military conflict is not America's greatest threat.

"Today more than one observer argues that the barbarians are not only coming but are over the drawbridge, across the moat and in the city," writes James Montgomery Boice in his book, *Two Cities, Two Loves.* "They have occupied every one of our contemporary citadels. The signs of the collapse of Western culture are on every hand."[1]

It is the internal rot — the disintegration within — that troubles me most.

Charles Colson, special counsel to President Richard Nixon from 1969 to 1973, writes in *Against the Night: Living in the New Dark Ages:*

> Today in the West, and particularly in America, the new barbarians are all around us. They are not hairy Goths and Vandals, swilling fermented brew and ravishing maidens; they are not Huns and Visigoths storming our borders or scaling our city walls. No, this time the invaders have come from within. We have bred them in our families and trained them in our classrooms. They inhabit our legislatures, our courts, our film studios, and our churches. Most of them are attractive and pleasant; their ideas are persuasive and subtle. These men and women threaten our most cherished institutions and our very character as a people.[2]

The evidence mounts for the presence of these cultural "barbarians" in the circles Colson mentions: our families, churches, government, and schools.

WHO NEEDS MOM AND DAD?

The virtual collapse of the family in one generation produced ripple effects from the cradle to the classroom and from the schoolhouse to the marketplace. The facts speak for themselves:

■ One million children live through the breakup of the family.

■ Ten million children live in one-parent families.

■ Children are taught to question authority, rules, and "conventional" answers. Outcome-based education and Goals 2000 continue to reinforce this philosophy.

■ Revisionist history has stolen our children's past; humanist educators have ostracized God; "how-to" sex education classes have stripped children of their modesty; and self-esteem has been elevated to the ultimate goal.

■ Our education system, basically run by the National Education Association (NEA), has left our children with no foundations and no future. Moreover, through the NEA's endorsement, homosexuals have emerged from the closet and are flaunting their lifestyle in the classroom.

■ Homosexuals are trying to infiltrate the Boy Scouts of America. At least one local troop has succumbed.

■ The Justice Department claims there are over 120,000 gang members in 1,436 gangs nationwide.[3]

The erosion of family life has weakened the fiber of our nation and reduced its capacity to withstand the inrush of evil threatening our future.

"Ordained by God as the basic unit of human organization," Charles Colson writes, "the family is not only necessary for propagation of the race, but is the first school of human instruction. Parents take small self-centered monsters who spend much of their time screaming defiantly and hurling peas on the carpet and teach them to share, to wait their turn, to respect others' property. These lessons translate into respect for others, self-restraint, obedience to the law — in short, into the virtues of individual character that are vital to a society's survival."[4]

**We don't need more police.
We need more mothers and fathers.**

When Gary, Indiana was cited as leading the nation in homicides per capita (1966), Dwight Gardner, a professor at Indiana University-Northwest, said, "The problems are in the homes and the families that need to be reconstructed. We don't need more police. We need more mothers and fathers."[5]

I can't help but wonder: Where were mom and dad the day a brother shot his pre-teen sister because she overheard him making a drug deal on the phone? Where were the parents of the boys who threw two pre-schoolers out a fifth-floor window of their tenement building?

THE COMING CRIME WAVE

The indications of decay are everywhere. Most Americans, however, are not only oblivious to the extent of our problems but are unaware of the cause as well.

When popular talk show hostess Laura Schlessinger was asked if America was in a moral crisis, she answered, "Totally! When you get somebody like me who is simply saying there are moral ways of handling things, and I can get attacked for it, you know we have a moral crisis."

Once in a while the alarm is so shrill and insistent that we find it difficult to roll over and go back to sleep.

Of growing concern is the "predicted mother of all crime waves." According to the recently published *Body Count: Moral Poverty and How to Win America's War against Crime and Drugs,* a new generation of "super-predators," untouched by any moral inclinations, will hit America's streets in the next decade.

John DiIulio, Jr. of the Brookings Institute who co-wrote *Body Count* with W. Bennett and John Walters, calls it a "multivariate phenomenon," meaning that child abuse, the high number of available high-tech guns, alcoholism, and many other factors feed the problem.[6]

University of Pennsylvania professor Marvin Wolfgang notes these tragic statistics:

■ Six to seven percent of the boys in an age group will be chronic offenders, meaning they are arrested five or more times before the age of 18.

■ There will be 500,00 more boys ages 14 to 17 in the year 2000 than there were in 1995.

■ There will be at least 30,000 more youth criminals on the streets.

■ Between 1990 and 2010, there will be 4.5 million more boys, yielding 270,000 young criminals.

"The big destruction happens early," Heritage Foundation fellow Pat Fagan says. "By the age of four or five, the kid is really warped. Psychologists can predict by the age of six who'll be the super-predators."

How does a pre-schooler become warped?

"Child abuse and alcohol ruin these children," Fagan explains. "But the groundwork was laid three decades ago with the widespread adoption of birth control, which made the sexual revolution possible. It altered people's dedication to their children and altered a fundamental orientation of society."

Evidence of our diminished moral values was illustrated when two bright, popular college students from well-to-do families solved the problem of an unwanted pregnancy by wrapping the six-pound, two-ounce newborn and throwing it in the garbage. The medical examiner says the baby was born alive but died from "blunt-force head trauma and shaking."

How could it happen? Columnist Mona Charen answers:

In the name of "choice," we have dulled the conscience of this nation almost beyond recognition. When the President of the United States defends a procedure that sucks the brains out of babies who are three-quarters born and fully capable of surviving on their own — and does so in the name of morality — is it really so surprising?

When *Roe vs. Wade* was decided, ethicists and theologians warned that we had taken the disastrous first step toward devaluing all human life. That has been accomplished. The infant has no intrinsic value.

A schoolmate of the couple told the *New York Post*, "They are both really popular, smart and everything. They were just in a bad situation."

Judy Mellen, executive director of the Delaware chapter of the American Civil Liberties Union, was outraged that prosecutors were seeking the death penalty. "These kids are not criminals," she said. By the standards of Bill Clinton's America, Miss Mellen is probably right. These are not criminals; these are just kids with a poor sense of timing. Their tragedy is that they imbibed moral confusion from the likes of the ACLU and the President of the United States while the criminal code of the state of Delaware still rests upon the Ten Commandments.[7]

How far have we fallen when two morally bankrupt teenagers can murder an innocent newborn and be labeled "kids in a bad situation"? Come on. These were intelligent college kids. If they didn't want the baby, all they had to do was go to the Yellow Pages and find at least a dozen organizations willing to help them.

The truth is, they believed the pro-choice lie and considered the baby to be so much garbage — especially in light of their personal goals and plans.

IS ANYBODY HOME?

Too often the social planners and opinion makers haven't a clue as to the nature of the crisis or the safeguards God has provided to protect human life. Surely our Maker knows the best way to uphold the sanctity of marriage, insure the security of our homes, and protect the children born into those families.

But man thinks he knows better. Notice for example the spin offered to justify the diminishing role of mothers.

Will parents cherish their children at home or let the state raise them in day cares?

According to *USA Today,* a recent survey has shown that day care is not harmful to the growth or bonding of a child. "Day care before age three doesn't hinder children's mental development or weaken their emotional bond with their mothers."

"These are heartwarming findings," says psychologist Sarah Freidman, the study's scientific coordinator, of the National Institute of Child Health and Human Development.

Heartwarming for who? The mothers? If the kids could talk they might have a different opinion.

Then, almost as an afterthought, the survey says, "The more hours a child spends at day care, the less sensitively mom relates to him by age three and the less socially engaged he is with his mother."

In other words, the mother-child bond is seriously jeopardized. What impact does this lack of motherly contact have on the child?

According to British psychiatrist John Bowlby — well-known for his theory of attachment — the attachment relationship that a young child forges with his mother "forms the foundation stone of personality."

Bowlby writes in his book, *Attachment and Loss,* that "the young child's hunger for his mother's presence is as great as his hunger for food . . . and that her absence inevitably generates a powerful sense of loss and anger."[8]

Raymond S. Moore, developmental psychologist, former college president, and U. S. Office of Education official, has done extensive research in early institutionalization of young children. He warned:

We conclude that our only reasonable chance for survival as a free democracy is to educate parents on the value of cherishing their children longer in the homes. As we look at modern trends, with millions both in day care and in nursing homes, we are compelled to conclude that the earlier you institutionalize your children, the earlier they will institutionalize you.[9]

Still the attack on the home and family continues. First Lady Hillary Clinton is pushing the UN Convention on the Rights of the Child. This "new" concept proclaims that the government should "protect children from the power of parents."

Rosaline Bush, editor of *Family Voice*, tells of a young boy who reported being paddled by his parents. A school counselor in Texas contacted the Children's Protective Service (CPS). The CPS came to the school, where they forced the child to strip in front of female officials — to check for "child abuse." When the parents filed suit, a federal district court judge in Houston ruled that "parents lose their rights to direct the upbringing of their children when they put their children in public school."[10]

Did you get that? You, as a parent, give up all rights to little Susie and Tommy when they enter the doors of your local public school!

The barbarians are not only over the drawbridge, across the moat and in the city; they've broken down the picket fence and entered the parlor.

PAGANS IN THE PEWS

Even the house of God has not been spared the infection of unbelief. From New York to California, the poison taints the bloodstream.

Judson Memorial Church in Greenwich Village, named after the first American missionary, Adoniram Judson, has long since abandoned the faith. The sanctuary, where believers once sat to hear the gospel preached, is now an auditorium where people come to view nude plays.

Unbelief and a disregard for the Scriptures have infected the Church.

In Glide Memorial Church in San Francisco, where Gypsy Smith once called sinners to repentance, the Rev. Cecil Williams has garnered national headlines for its unorthodox blending of rock music, light shows, and its own version of "liberation theology."

When questioned about moral issues, Rev. Williams said, "I guess the important thing with me is that I don't become a captive to the Scriptures. . . . I know somebody will say this is the inspired Word of God. But who has that kind of direct pipeline? Nobody?"[11]

Rev. George Matheson had that kind of direct access and was happy to live under divine authority.

In one of his hymns he has this line, "Make me a captive, Lord, and then I shall be free."

In *Paul's Attitude to Scripture,* E. Earle Ellis tells how an admirer once said to Adolph Schlatter, the renowned New Testament scholar, that he had always wanted to meet a theologian like him who stood upon the Word of God. Schlatter replied, "Thank you, but I don't stand on the Word of God; I stand under it."

Ellis comments, "He wasn't quibbling about prepositions. The distinction he made is a crucial one, and it goes to the heart of our discipleship as servants of the Word."[12]

James Montgomery Boice writes:

Evangelicals have abandoned a proper commitment to revealed truth and have become mere pragmatists. Instead of proclaiming and teaching God's truth, the Bible, they are resorting to sermonettes of pop psychology, entertainment-style services and technological approaches to church growth, which is a formula not for the increase of true religion but the end of it. Evangelical churches are growing, but they no longer have anything distinct to offer. They are popular in many places, but the prophetic, challenging voice of the Christian preacher and teacher, which has been the glory and strength of the church in all past ages, has been lost.[13]

No wonder our homes are filled with discord, our streets are chaotic with disorder, our jails are full, and our moral capital is spent. When a trumpet gives an uncertain sound, the troops twist and turn in labyrinthine circles rather than march straight ahead to certain victory.

WAITING FOR LIGHT

Revealed religion is the fountainhead; the whole civilization issues from this source.

When Mario Cuomo, New York's ex-governor, spoke to a group of young people in Minneapolis, he apologized for leaving the world in such a mess. "It's the fault of my generation," he said. Then he made a significant statement: "We have left you with no single given belief you could put your fingers on."[14]

Absent that "single given belief," nothing remains but a moral relativism, a makeshift platform upon which to stand.

Larry King, veteran broadcaster, was asked, "If you could ask God one question, what would it be?"

"Did you have a Son?" King replied.[15]

It is our solemn responsibility and glorious privilege to proclaim with certainty, "God does have a Son! He came once to die for our sins, and He's coming again to reign on the earth."

A Seattle minister, however, describes his journey from a "born again" experience in his youth to the loss of faith at Yale Divinity School. "Under the guidance of scholarly professors," he writes, "kindly classmates and loving friends, I came to see Christianity in a new light."

The truth is, he abandoned the faith. He says he came to believe that "the study of the Scriptures reveals to me that Jesus did not believe himself to be God.... Jesus did not die to justify us before God.... As for the resurrection, whether it was 'spiritual' or 'physical,' who can say? I place this concept on a shelf titled 'waiting for light.'"[16]

The apostle Paul said, "If Christ is not risen, then our preaching is in vain" (1 Cor. 15:14).

When the German poet and dramatist Goethe lay dying, he whispered, "More light. More light."

It's best not to wait until you're dying to be sure about the resurrection.

Unbelievers in the pulpits, infidels at the lecterns, skeptics in the seminaries, pagans in the pews — and blood in the streets.

The scourge of Nazism and Communism, which bathed this planet in blood and tears, traces its origins to a church or lecture hall where the noxious breath of unbelief blew out the light of truth.

■ Charles Darwin, who popularized the theory of evolution, which undermined biblical values and the concept of ultimate truth, studied theology at Cambridge University.

■ Adolf Hitler received religious training as a boy.

■ Karl Marx, though Jewish, was baptized in a Christian church.

■ Joseph Stalin, singly responsible for the slaughter of tens of millions, studied for the priesthood.

Did any of the aforementioned sit under the influence of a man of God who believed that Jesus is the living Christ? Or were they confirmed in their lostness under the baneful tutelage of preachers and professors who had placed the subject of the resurrection on a shelf titled, "Waiting for light"?

**It's best not to wait until you're dying
to be sure about the resurrection.**

BACK TO BONDAGE?

Newsweek columnist Meg Greenfield wrote:

People in Washington don't say, "The devil made me do it" anymore. They say, "I asked the ethics office, and they said it didn't fall within the category of impermissible activity." Or, more frequently, when there is a flap about something that has already occurred, they say, "We have directed the ethics office to look into it and report back to us in 60 days." Good old "60 days" — for something that your ordinary, morally sentient person wouldn't need 60 seconds to figure out."[17]

Perhaps our shabby conduct can be attributed to a loss of identity. We don't know who we are.

Is America a Christian nation? Yes, according to the Supreme Court. In *Church of the Holy Trinity vs. United States* (143 US 457, 36L ed. 226), the Supreme Court in 1891 issued the following declaration:

> Our laws and our institutions must necessarily be based upon and embody the teachings of the Redeemer of Mankind. It is impossible that it should be otherwise; and in this sense and to this extent our civilization and our institutions are emphatically Christian . . . this is a religious people. This is historically true. From the discovery of this continent to the present hour, there is a single voice making this affirmation . . . this is a Christian nation.[18]

We would do well to dismiss the historical revisionists, go back and dust off the foundation of this good land, and renew our acquaintance with the God of our fathers. If we don't, we may very well go the way of other great world powers.

Toward the end of the 18th century, Alexander Fraser Tyler wrote that "a democracy cannot exist as a permanent form of government."

How long can a democracy last? "It can only exist until the voters discover that they can vote themselves money from the Treasury," Tyler noted. "From that moment on the majority always votes for the candidates promising the most benefits from the Public Treasury, with the result that a democracy always collapses over loose fiscal policy followed by dictatorship."

How long does this process take? "The average age of the world's greatest civilizations has been 200 years," according to Tyler.

Interestingly, Tyler discovered that these nations all progressed through the same sequence:

From bondage to spiritual faith
From spiritual faith to great courage
From courage to liberty
From liberty to abundance
From abundance to selfishness
From selfishness to complacency
From complacency to apathy
From apathy to dependency
From dependency back into bondage.[19]

It is not difficult to conclude that America is well on its way through that cycle. The day is far spent, the night is at hand.

How do we know? The signs of the times signal disaster as Tal Brooke, president of the Berkeley-based Spiritual Counterfeits Project, Inc. points out:

The nation that once shone with virtue, wanting to revere God in its beginning, is daring

God with defiant public spectacles that repudiate every pillar the nation once stood upon — from in-your-face gay pride parades and homosexual and lesbian solidarity marches, pro-abortion rallies, feminist and anti-family events, to national celebrations of the godhood of man and the divinity of nature. Dolphins have more rights than babies in the womb. Drugs pollute the national bloodstream.

Many families lie in tatters, with men and women at odds. And of course, the national treasury has been empty for a long time.[20]

The emptiness of the national treasury is a scandal, but no less serious is the poverty of our moral resources. Nowhere is this seen more clearly than in our schools.

"From the discovery of this continent to the present hour, there is a single voice making this affirmation . . . this is a Christian nation."

BARBARIANS IN THE CLASSROOM

By near unanimous consent, our educational system is a shambles. Schools have become jungles or — as James Montgomery Boice calls them — "training centers for barbarism in which old barbarians teach young barbarians to be even more barbarous than those who preceded them."[21]

Teachers — most of whom entered the profession with the highest ideals — weary of undisciplined students and struggling without encouragement from administrators and parents, count the days until the pension kicks in. Most are good teachers caught in a bad situation.

Presidential candidate Bob Dole promised if elected to build a bridge to the past. President Bill Clinton offered to build a bridge to the future.

A bridge to the past is essential, for as George Orwell said, "Who controls the past, controls the future."

Novelist Saul Bellow claims the Jewish culture would never have survived without the stories that give meaning to the Jewish moral tradition. And a bridge to the future is required to link the values and traditions of an earlier day with hope and promise of a future day.

Most of all, however, we need a bridge to the truth.

Christina Hoff Sommers writes, "We may be one of the few societies in the world that finds itself incapable of passing on its moral teachings to young people."[22]

Sommers wrote an article titled *Ethics Without Virtue,* in which she discussed abortion, euthanasia, capital punishment, DNA research, and the ethics of transplant surgery while pointing out that students learn almost nothing about "private decency, honesty, personal responsibility, or honor."

A colleague ridiculed the article, saying, unlike Sommers, she would continue to focus on social issues of social justice, women's oppression, corruption in big business, the power of government, transgressions of multinational corporations in the Third World countries.

Toward the end of the semester, the socially focused teacher came in looking chagrined.

"What's wrong?" Sommers asked.

"The students cheated on their social justice take-home finals. They plagiarized!"

Apparently, more than half of the students in the ethics class had copied long passages from the secondary literature.

"What are you going to do?" Christina Sommers asked.

"Could I see your article again?" the teacher replied.[23]

If we have nothing to teach, if "there are no correct answers," if ethics is doing what is right at the time — then the expenditure of additional funds will do little to solve the problems we face in education.

John Silber, president of Boston University, asserts, "We must dispel the myth that we can improve our educational system simply by spending more money on it. This is a demonstrable falsehood, and yet we subscribe to it over and over again at great cost to the taxpayer, and at far greater cost to the quality of our children's education."[24]

Newt Gingrich notes the deterioration of our nation's moral priorities in the last few years:

> It is impossible to maintain civilization with 12-year-olds having babies, 15-year-olds killing each other, 17-year-olds dying of AIDS, or 18-year-olds getting diplomas they can't read. . . .
>
> It is a grand irony, because we managed to contain the Soviet Empire for half a century, win an enormous victory for freedom, and in the same cycle begin the process of decaying our civilization.[25]

What a sad diagnosis of our nation's social and spiritual condition.

MEN WITHOUT A PAST

A visit to the nation's capital must include the Jefferson Memorial and the Holocaust Museum.

Adjacent to the Tidal Basin, the Jefferson Memorial — a magnificent circular structure — surrounds a giant statue of our third president. Excerpts from his speeches and writings are inscribed on the walls, including this profound statement:

> God Who gave us life gave us liberty. Can the liberties of a nation be secure when we have

removed the conviction that these liberties are the gift of God? Indeed, I tremble for my country when I reflect that God is just.

Every good thing we enjoy is a direct result of our covenant relationship with God. It is not by accident or coincidence that we are the most richly endowed people on earth.

Opened in 1993, the Holocaust Museum commemorates the six million Jews who died in Hitler's death camps. The haunting words of Adolf Hitler quoted at the museum sharply diverge from those of Thomas Jefferson, "I want to raise a generation of young people who are devoid of conscience, imperious, relentless, and cruel."[26]

The stark contrast between the two world views is both chilling and instructive.

**A revolution cannot succeed
until you have separated the youth
from their roots.**

What are we doing to preserve the idea that economic, political, and religious freedom flows from spiritual liberty? What price will we pay if we don't?

It is the duty of a society to pass on its moral teachings to the next generation. Failure to do so leads to "a rootless society, unaware of where we came from or the price that was paid for our freedom."

George Roche, president of Hillsdale College, writes, "Men without a past are forever children easily manipulated and easily enslaved."[27]

A revolution cannot succeed until you have separated the youth from their roots. Hitler understood this, and he employed the techniques of brainwashing and propaganda to lead Europe's' most civilized nation to ruin.

NO CRIME TO KILL

On a recent trip to Europe, we left our hotel one morning and drove a few miles down the road to a Polish village, then two or three miles farther until we came to Auschwitz, the largest of the scores of Nazi death camps. Auschwitz, the awful word is linked with Dachau, Treblinka, Bergen-Belsen, Buchenwald, and others, where man's inhumanity to man plummeted to new depths.

During the hours of that unforgettable day, we walked through the rooms of a human hell, "witnessing spectacle after spectacle of the depths to which the human mind descends when conscience dies."[28]

Many of the barracks still stand, stark and grim, where human beings were warehoused, tortured, beaten, starved. We saw the wall against which hapless victims were lined up to be shot, and the gallows where they were hanged. In the cellar stands the table where Dr. Mengele performed experiments on living human beings — twins were his specialty.

And the gas chambers. This was the end for women and children — and men too weak to work. Packed to capacity, the doors were sealed and pellets of Cyclon-B gas were dropped from an opening in the ceiling. It took long, agonizing minutes to die.

When the screams died away and the gasping and clawing and struggling ceased, the doors were opened, hoses were brought to suck out the gas, and the bodies were dragged to the ovens.

A worker at Auschwitz said that "the stench given off by the pyres contaminated the surrounding countryside at night. The red sky over Auschwitz could be seen for miles."

Every 24 hours, twelve to fifteen thousand men, women, and children were reduced to ashes, and night and day the gray, greasy smoke curled up from the chimneys — a silent testimony to the madness of a man who said, "I do not consider Jews to be animals. They are further removed from the animals than we are; therefore, it is no crime to exterminate them since they are not a part of humanity at all."[29]

Following cremation, a handful of ashes was placed in a box, labeled with the number of a victim, and for a payment of 50 marks delivered to the families.

CLUES TO THE HOLOCAUST

Eli Wiesel, who later won the Nobel Peace Prize, lived happily with his family in a small Hungarian village until the Nazis came in 1944. The Jews were ordered from their homes, driven to the center of the city, and loaded onto cattle cars.

Young Eli last saw his mother and little sister when they got off the cars at Auschwitz. He and his father survived for several months until shortly before liberation when they were herded like cattle to Buchenwald, where he watched as his father was murdered.

Years later, testifying at the trial of a former SS guard, Wiesel described the hell through which he had passed:

We watched as our world was systematically narrowed. For Jews the country was limited to one town. The town to one neighborhood. The neighborhood to one street. The street to a sealed boxcar crossing the Polish countryside at night.[30]

Across the electric fence and razor wire, within a stone's throw of this place of horror, in an elegant three-story house surrounded by flowers and gardens, lived the commandant of Auschwitz, Rudolph Hoess, with his wife and children. Few creature comforts were denied the family. On one occasion, Mrs. Hoess said, "I could live here till I die."

Here? Where men were tortured, women raped, children thrown into the air and shot? Here where a million-and-a-half Jews were murdered?

Is this the millennium Adolf Hitler promised? And who was this madman who rescued Germany from defeat in World War I only to destroy it on the blood-soaked battlefields of three continents in World War II? The proud and glorious Third Reich, built to last a thousand years, perished in the flames of its burning cities after 12 years, four months and eight days.

How could it have happened? How could the most Christian nation of Europe produce such savagery? How could a nation that gave the world Beethoven and Bach give us a Himmler, a Goering, a Goebbels, a Hoess? How could the people who have contributed so much in literature, science, art, music, architecture, theology — a people who valued the university and loved libraries and museums and prided themselves on their culture — how could they give us a Hitler?

Victor Frankl, a Holocaust survivor, provides us a clue:

The gas chambers of Auschwitz were the ultimate consequence of the theory that man is nothing but the product of heredity and environment — or, as the Nazis like to say, "Of Blood and Soul." I'm absolutely convinced that the gas chambers of Auschwitz, Treblinka, and

Maidanek were ultimately prepared not in some
ministry or other in Berlin, but rather at the
desks and in the lecture halls of nihilistic scien-
tists and philosophers.[31]

Erwin Lutzer, pastor of Chicago's Moody Church,
declared that "such doctrines undercut the ability of
the church to stand against the atrocities of the Third
Reich. Substituting human ideas for the revelation of
God, the cross of Christ was reinterpreted to advance
a pagan agenda."[32]

Can it happen again? No one is better qualified to
answer that question that Eli Wiesel:

Over the years I have often put the question to
my young students. And they, consistently,
have answered yes, while I said no. I saw it as
a unique event that would remain unique. I
believed that if mankind had learned anything
from it, it was that hate and murder reach beyond the direct participants; he who begins by
killing another, in the end will kill his own. . . .

I was wrong. What happened once, could
happen again. Perhaps I am exaggerating.
Perhaps I am oversensitive. But then I belong to
a traumatized generation. We have learned to
take threats more seriously than promises.[33]

A tall, muscular, handsome gentleman came to me
after a speaking engagement, shook my hand, and

said, "You just shook the hand that shook Adolf Hitler's hand."

He told me he had been a Hitler youth as a boy, and remembers the day Hitler visited the camp.

What was the Fuhrer's blueprint for world power? Stifle the Christian church, take over the education function, start with the children.

IDEAS AND CONSEQUENCES

Ideas have consequences — that is what I hope to convey in this book.

The consequences of ideas are apparent throughout history. Jefferson or Hitler, which will it be?

The passion, the purpose, the principles of the Founding Fathers, enunciated in their sacred documents and demonstrated in unwavering commitment to those principles, resulted in a parade of opportunities never before experienced by people anywhere.

The consequences of ideas are apparent throughout history. Jefferson or Hitler, which will it be?

By contrast, the philosophy of Nazism — a veritable witch's brew of ideas — the unbelief of Feurbach, the statism of Hegel, the evolution of Darwin, the nihilism of Nietzsche, the racism of Chamberlain, the hatred of Hitler. Where did their ideas lead? To the enslavement of nations and the slaughter of their people.

These very "philosophies" are applauded and taught in the schools, colleges, and universities of America today. And who is caught in the cross hairs? Your children. (Not to mention that your tax dollars are funding the coming carnage.)

It makes little difference how firm the foundation, how tall the skyscrapers, how advanced the technology, how mighty the military, how magnificent the cities, how fertile the fields, how soothing the music, how robust the sports, how erudite the teachers, how brilliant the students — if we are educated beyond our intelligence, ever learning but never able to come to the knowledge of the truth, disregarding the moral law and disavowing the moral Lawgiver.

The fact remains: The greatest, richest, and freest nation in history faces a destruction that will dwarf the plunder of Rome and rival the bombing of Dresden and the burning of Hamburg.

Hyperbole? Exaggeration? Maybe. But remember the proud passenger on the Titanic who boasted, "God Himself could not sink this ship."

CHAPTER FOUR

Sights and Sounds of Decadence

A young man with a trance-like stare and glazed eyes sat in my office and described the rock concert he had attended the night before.

"The music was so loud I couldn't hear a thing," he said. "Man, it was wonderful."

That brings to mind Evelyn Waugh, who, writing late in life, stated, "I am quite deaf now; such comfort."

Newsweek described a raucous event that might have been even more deafening:

An electric guitar's high-pitched note comes crashing down in a pulsating rhythm as the bass loudly kicks in. Mesmerized, the small club's mostly young, mostly male audience chants with fists clenched in the air.

"The music gets you into such a frenzy that you want to jump around, dive off the stage," says Chris Williams, head of Rock Hotel Productions. "I had a kid come up to me and say, 'I had such a good time, I broke my arm.'"[1]

MTV senior vice president and general manager, Lee Masters, describes the devotees of this kind of music. "You won't find a more loyal following," he says. "They're maniacs."

What better customer than a maniac? No wonder the entertainment industry does everything possible to exploit America's children. In fact, they purposely appeal to young people through music that defies and subverts authority of any kind.

Judge Bork supplies the method behind the madness:

An impresario who developed one star after another was asked how he did it. He said, "I look for someone their parents will hate."

As Professor Todd Gitlin notes, the blues had been music for adults, but rock was about teenage problems. Its "incoherence, primitive regression, was indeed part of the music's appeal" to the young.

Gerald Howard wrote: "Rock 'n' roll, a raw and powerful new form of music, crystallized all the youthfulness, dynamism, and hypersexuality on the loose — the Pied Piper's tune of the new freedoms."[2]

Judge Bork calls this "an apt metaphor" since the historical Pied Piper "led the children into the forest, where he massacred and dismembered them."

Who should be held responsible for the carnage among America's youth? "The record company executives, the new robber barons, who mine gold out of rock," writes Bork — an activity that "has all the moral dignity of drug trafficking."

The entertainment industry purposely appeals to young people through music that defies and subverts authority of any kind.

Robert Bork warns Americans: "We are living through a cultural collapse, and major corporations are presiding over that collapse and grabbing everything they can on the way down."[3]

PREMIER MARKETER OF FILTH

One of the corporations "grabbing everything they can" and getting rich at the expense of your kids is Time-Warner, the premier marketer of filth. John Leo called Time-Warner "our leading cultural polluter."

D. DeLores Tucker, a Democrat and head of the National Political Congress of Black Women, and William Bennett, former secretary of education and drug czar, met with the top executives of Time-Warner to protest the practice.

Robert Bork describes the meeting:

Tucker passed copies of the lyrics of Nine Inch Nails' "Big Man With a Gun" to the Time-Warner executives and asked them to read the words aloud. None of them would. One of the Tucker-Bennett party did read out the words and asked if the executives found the lyrics offensive.

The discussion included modern liberal gems from Time-Warner as, "Art is difficult to interpret," "What is art?" and "Who decides what is pornography?"

Bennett answered: "The answers are simple. To the first question: 'Big Man With a Gun' is as easy to interpret as an obscenity scrawled in a public lavatory; to the second: whatever art may be, this isn't it; and to the third: the public acting through its designated representatives can decide."[4]

Bennett asked the executives, "Is there anything so low, so bad, that you will not sell it?"

A long silence followed.

In response to their vapid answers, Bennett said "baloney" a couple of times. At that point, Time-Warner's chairman, Gerald M. Levin, objected to such language and walked out of the meeting.

This is the same Mr. Levin whose recording "artists" use vulgarity, profanity, and blasphemy to warp the minds of your children. And believe me, the impact is far from a bunch of baloney.

"Though students do not have books, they most emphatically do have music," Allan Bloom wrote in *The Closing of the American Mind*. He also noted:

> Nothing is more singular about this generation than its addiction to music. This is the age of music and the state of the soul that accompany it. . . . Today, a very large proportion of young people between the ages of 10 and 20 live for music. It is their passion; nothing else excites them; they cannot take seriously anything alien to music — it is available 24 hours a day, everywhere — even while studying.[5]

Growing up with Guy Lombardo and Glen Miller, I may be too old to appreciate the screaming guitars and pulsating rhythm of today's music. Then again, my absence at the concerts may be a matter of self-preservation; I don't want to end up a stone-deaf maniac with a broken arm.

TIME AND TELEVISION

It is not only music to which this generation is addicted. Technology has introduced a brave new world of sights and sounds leaving little time to be alone or to be quiet. The sound of silence is deafening to people who were nursed on noise, brought up on a cacophony of sounds, desensitized by flickering images, and entertained beyond the experience of any people who ever lived.

How does all this continuous barrage of the senses affect a young mind? Consider the pervasive influence of television as described by E. Lonnie Melashenko in *The Television Time Bomb:*[6]

■ Television consumes up to one-half of a child's waking hours with passive inactivity that could be spent in achievement — and achievement is the surest road to self-esteem.

Television is the most important educational institution in the United States today.
— **John Silber**

■ The average child spends 28 hours a week watching TV and four hours playing video games, but spends only 30 minutes a week alone with Dad, 2.5 hours alone with Mom, five hours doing homework, and two hours reading.

■ Robert McNeil estimates that the average watcher spends 10,000 hours in front of the television set for each decade of life. "Ten thousand hours," McNeil adds, "is enough time for a high school graduate to earn a Ph.D."

■ Michael Medved, film critic, says the average child will spend more time in front of the television screen before he is six than he will spend talking to his father the rest of his life.

As the major storyteller to America's children, television not only determines what stories will be told but also what lessons will be learned.

Boston University president, John Silber, goes even further. He concludes, "Television is the most important educational institution in the United States today, and within a few years it will be the most important educational force in all free societies."[7]

It's not just the investment of time — or waste of time — it is the effect of the music and television programming that is alarming.

Maybe Michael Medved has a point when he says, "The major problem with the media today isn't too much sex, or too much violence, or too much rude behavior; it is too much TV, period."

TV'S SEX EDUCATORS

A groundbreaking study by Monique Ward, a postdoctoral fellow at the University of California at Los Angeles, tracked and analyzed sexual content in 1992-93 prime-time shows most popular among youngsters two to 12 and 12 to 17. On average, 29 percent of all interactions involved sex talk of some kind.

"Sex," Ms. Ward notes, "is most often depicted as a competition, a way to define masculinity, and an 'exciting amusement for people of all ages.'"[8]

Jane Brown, a professor in the school of journalism and mass communications at the University of North Carolina at Chapel Hill, says, "I think of the media as our true sex educators."

Children Now, an Oakland, California advocacy group, polled 750 children ages 10 to 16. The study showed, "Six out of 10 said sex on TV sways kids to have sex at too young an age."

Do you want your children to learn misconceptions about sex? Just let them watch prime time TV.

With 25 talk show hosts competing for about 100 hours of programs weekly, producers must shamelessly reach to the bottom of the barrel for themes that will titillate a jaded audience, such as: "Women who marry their rapists," and another about mothers and daughters having affairs with the same man.

"In one Richard Bey outing, Karen admitted she had offered her husband to Donna as a sleeping companion; Carolyn, who said her brother had slept with her boyfriend; and Geena, who said she had slept with an old friend's fiancé. Geena presented her old friend with a birthday cake on stage before confessing to her, and got the cake back in her face. The audience whooped."

Such antics by adults — and the audience's applause of such crude behavior — send a debilitating message to children: This is normal and acceptable behavior.

Then there are the soaps.

Millions of Americans not only view the mindless soaps but buy magazines that review the fictional goings-on of the mythical characters. While adults sit in slavish bondage to the daily melodramas, children and teens watch right along with them, taking in every steamy, bedroom scene in full color.

"We believe we can treat sexuality purely in terms of consumer demand and that this will have no consequences," notes John Silber. "We believe that we can permit television to portray sex without responsibility — no fault sex — at frequent intervals day and night."[9]

Even more tragic is the fact that parents see nothing wrong with exposing innocent minds to such explicit — and ungodly — behavior.

Things have changed in the last 50 years since television's invention and increasing invasion into American family life. John Silber makes this disturbing observation:

Only a generation or two ago, society as a whole and parents in particular recognized that there is a period in human development when overt sexuality is inappropriate and positively harmful. Parents then went out of their way to protect children from premature exposure to sex. Today, even if they wish to protect them, how can they?[10]

Monitoring and censoring your child's viewing is not an easy task, but it can be done. To exert no control is to hand your child's mind over to be manipulated — and possibly destroyed — by the monster sitting in your living room.

COAST TO COAST BEHAVIOR MODIFICATION

A study by the American Psychiatric Association figures that the typical child, watching 27 hours of TV a week, will view 8,000 murders, and 100,000 acts of violence from age three to 12.

"Americans have the dubious distinction of being the first culture to passively submit themselves and their children to a coast-to-coast and lifelong process of mass behavior modification via an electronic hookup in their homes,"[11] writes author David R. Mains.

How is our behavior modified? By barraging us with action-packed thrillers of fast-paced car chases, blown up buildings, and machine gun stand-offs in which the heroes walk away unscathed.

Reality, of course, takes a back seat and real-life consequences seldom make the screen. Have you ever noticed that after a violent encounter, no one is ever shown to be maimed or injured or paralyzed for life? Instead, the poor victims are sanitarily blown to bits, leaving no trace of their mangled bodies.

The increase in violent programming has created a culture of disrespect that has redefined how we are supposed to treat one another.

Does television present an accurate picture of real American life? Not according to recent findings:

- Crime is portrayed in television about 55 times more often than it occurs in real life.
- The specific crime of murder is portrayed at nearly 1,000 times its real-world rate.

And we wonder at the growing trend toward violent acts by teens and even younger children.

The increase in violent programming has created a culture of disrespect that has redefined how we are supposed to treat one another. In fact, violence is the epitome of disrespect.

Children — and adults — are being desensitized to evil. How? By being conditioned to first tolerate, then enjoy, violence so hideous that it is naturally repugnant and even nauseating to someone who has never been exposed to television.

Behavior therapists tell us that values can be quickly extinguished through a method known as "systematic desensitization."

WHERE ARE THE CHRISTIANS?

On television, almost no one goes to church — except for weddings and funerals. Yet, according to a January 1992 issue of *Newsweek,* 40 percent of Americans attend worship service weekly — five times as many as attend movie theaters in a week.

In real life, 90 percent of Americans identified themselves with Christianity.

On the screen, almost no continuing television series placed in a modern-day setting has a normal person portrayed as a Christian. When a TV movie is made about a Christian personality, he or she is presented as a money-grabbing, self-righteous bigot.

Some network programming has attempted to take a more positive approach with series like "Touched By an Angel," "Promised Land," and "Early Edition." Instead of macho type heroes, actors portray real-life good guys who solve everyday problems with good deeds — and sometimes even prayer!

Television news programs add to the confusion. If a well-known, professed Christian is interviewed, his motives are questioned and his beliefs belittled. It is disheartening to see godly, honorable men like Dan Quayle, Pat Robertson, Justice Clarence Thomas — to name a few — made out to be intolerant extremists with some hidden agenda.

On a recent national day of prayer, when hundreds of thousands of Americans gathered in homes and sanctuaries and courthouse squares to pray, the networks failed to appear. But let ten idiots gather downtown to protest the wanton killing of some protected species of flies or snails, and the cameras and news vans race to the scene.

One of the biggest news events of the week occurs every Sunday morning. Did you know that more people attend church on any given Sunday than attend all sporting events during the entire year combined? Now, that's real life!

Did you know that more people attend church on any given Sunday than attend all sporting events during the entire year combined?

THE MEDIUM *AND* THE MESSAGE

Beyond the waste of time and the harmful effects of many television programs, consider the *nature* of television. What does that mean? Remember Marshall McLuhan's famous quote, "The medium is the message"?

Jeffrey Hart explains why the medium of television has a negative impact no matter what your children watch. He explains it this way:

It would not matter if children watched "Sesame Street" or some such enlightened show all day long. The damage is done by the medium itself.

The trouble with the medium is that it creates an entirely passive viewer. The child sits there watching the images flicker and wash over them. What happens on the screen in no way engages the brain. It requires no effort at all on the part of the viewer. Indeed, it encourages a passive response to experience generally.[12]

What are the negative results of such passive behavior? Jeffrey Hart has found that "even undergraduates at elite colleges and universities seldom know how to read with patience and sustained critical attention."

Why is that? Because the average length of a shot on network television is only 9.5 seconds. This gives the eye no opportunity to rest; there is always something new to see.

In addition, few subjects are covered in-depth, leaving the viewer unable to question any facts presented. One program usually covers a variety of simple subject matter so as not to bore the viewer or elicit his use of comprehension skills. Most TV programs have one goal in mind for their audience — emotional gratification. Such gratification, however, usually comes in a negative medium.

As far back as 1950 — in the early days of mass television — T. S. Elliott wrote about TV in a letter to the *Times of London.* "I have just returned from a visit to the United States," he said, "where I found only anxiety and apprehension about its effect [mentally, morally, and physically] upon small children."

Television viewing has a negative impact on our mind, senses, personality, potential — and the way we view life.

Dr. Eric Peper of San Francisco State conducted an experiment on the effect of television on the brain wave patterns of children:

The horror of television is that the information goes in, but we don't react to it. It goes directly into our memory pool — later we react to it, but we don't know what we're reacting to. We have trained ourselves not to react, but later on we do things without knowing why, or even where the impulses come from.[13]

We don't have to look far to identify in ourselves or our children the negative impact television viewing has on our mind, senses, personality, potential — and the way we view life.

Consider these adverse effects:

- Reduces attention span
- Dulls the mind
- Creates a culture of disrespect
- Drowns out the sensibilities
- Suppresses revulsion and abhorrence of sin and violence
- Teaches insolence and arrogance toward others
- Emphasizes superficial qualities such as looks, charm, and showmanship
- Brainwashes formerly held beliefs
- Glamorizes witchcraft and occult practices
- Reprograms the mind toward evil
- Conditions to tolerate, then enjoy violence
- Ridicules Christians and Christianity
- Blasphemes God and Jesus Christ

Is it any wonder the Russian-born scientist Vladimir Kosma Zworykin, largely responsible for the invention of television, on his ninety-second birthday expressed his disgust with the whole matter: "I would never let my children even come close to this thing."

ENTERTAINED AND UNDERINFORMED

B. Russell Holt in his review of the book, *Amusing Ourselves to Death,* by Neil Postman, a professor of communication arts and sciences at New York University, writes:

Postman has written a frightening book. . . .
Frightening because he maintains that television
has fundamentally changed our notion of truth
and our ideas of intelligence — and that eventually and almost inevitably it will determine not
only how we think and communicate but what
it is possible to think and communicate.[14]

Postman's premise is that we have most to fear
from television "when its aspirations are high and it
sets itself up to be a carrier of important cultural
conversations."

**Television . . . has altered the way
Americans view abortion, homosexuality,
euthanasia, and casual sex.**

Unfortunately, we are already there. Television, in
large part, has altered the way Americans view
abortion, homosexuality, euthanasia, and casual sex.
How? By portraying godly, pro-life, pro-family
Christians as intolerant, bigoted, self-righteous, and
cruel. On the other hand, Murphy Brown, Ellen, and
Dr. Kevorkian are paraded across our screens as
"courageous, sensitive, and open-minded."

At the same time, American television is devoted
entirely to supplying its audience with entertainment.
As a result, the distinctions between show business

and other aspects of society — politics, education, religion, and the news — have been blurred.

Today, TV news itself must be entertaining or most people won't watch it. Everything about a news show spells "entertainment" — from the exciting opening music and the friendly, attractive cast with their pleasant banter to the vivid film footage and computer generated graphics. All the hype and personality suggest that what we are about to see is important, honest, and accurate.

At the same time, viewers are kept from getting too emotionally involved. Why should we care if thousands of Rwandans are unaccounted for in the jungles of Central Africa or if Zaire is in the throes of a civil war? Just show us a few mangled bodies — not too many — and then finish off with a nice shot of an African sunset. After all, what we have just seen is no cause for weeping.

The networks vie for top billing as the "most watched" news program or the one awarded for "the most in-depth coverage." Instead of news, however, we are merely given the "information" they want us to know. How many reports have you seen on Christians being tortured, maimed, imprisoned, and crucified in the Sudan and other Arab nations?

To obtain unbiased reporting the viewer must seek out the facts from other news sources — conservative news magazines, talk radio, or Christian news programs. Few Americans, however, have the time — or desire — for extensive personal investigation of the facts — and the media knows it!

"I do not question the legal right of the media to anticipate and distort the news," writes John Silber. "I oppose censorship of any kind, direct or indirect. I simply wish to ask: Can democracy, which depends on a people soundly educated on complex issues, and on the clear expression of the will of the people, survive the current self-indulgence of the media?[15]

I doubt it.

HOW ABOUT YOU?

Would you invite a liberal, biased, anti-Christian newscaster into your home every night for dinner, knowing he — or she — was going to distort the truth, slant the facts, and misinform you on important issues — and all the while promote an agenda that flies in the face of everything you believe and hold dear?

Would you let a stranger sit in the corner of your living room blathering on and on about nothing — or spout off foul, filthy language? Would you permit a guest in your home to repeatedly take God's name in vain or use the precious name of Jesus as a swear word?

Would you sit idly by as friends tell off-color jokes and make suggestive remarks within ear-shot of your children — or yourself, for that matter? Would you invite your children into the bedrooms of strangers engaged in sexual activity right before their eyes?

You have probably answered no to these questions. But when the TV — or a video — dumps the same kind of garbage into your living room, do you merely wince and say, "That's terrible"?

You may agree that television is pervasive, persuasive, and too often perverse. You probably realize that most TV programs are based on the trivial and assault the senses with polluted scenes and words. But what are you doing about it?

Censorship is impossible. V-chips and regulations are of little value.

Many of the opinion makers, political leaders, and great thinkers of our time don't even own a television.

Getting rid of the television has been the answer for some — like former Gov. William Weld of Massachusetts, Rabbi Daniel Lapin, Michael Medved, David Wilkerson, David Mains, Willard Cantelon. In fact, many of the opinion makers, political leaders, and great thinkers of our time don't even own a television.

Russell Kirk, the brilliant conservative writer of some 27 books was considered something of an eccentric. Why? Because he didn't own a TV until late in his life.

Many people who work in the television and entertainment industry limit their children's viewing time — just as many public schools teachers place their children in private schools. What do they know?

If donating your TV set to Goodwill sounds too extreme, you can certainly set limits. Here are a few suggestions:

- No TV on school nights.
- Shut off the TV during meals.
- Watch TV no more than you pray.
- Watch a certain program; don't mindlessly "watch TV." Indiscriminate television viewing enables someone else to set the agenda.
- Check out educational programs that offer information on history, people, animals, etc.
- Place the TV in a separate room where it is not the main focus of attention.
- Remove the TV from your child's room. (Sixty percent of American children have a TV in their bedroom.)
- Don't use the TV as a babysitter. Don't let children watch it alone.

With the proper guidance, however, watching television can be a positive experience.

- Watch TV with your children so you can discuss issues and how they relate to your family's values.
- Take your child to the library to check out books. Then let him earn TV time by reading a certain number of chapters.
- Suggest your child read a classic. Then reward him by renting a video of the story.

Does the Bible have anything to say on the subject? How about this verse? "I will set nothing wicked before my eyes" (Psalm 101:3).

We would do well to make a similar commitment.

You can set limits on television viewing and turn it into a positive experience for your entire family.

THE LUXURY OF INTROSPECTION

Many young people have never experienced the exquisite pleasure of browsing in an old bookstore, discovering a treasure, buying it, reading it, underlining a significant sentence, writing one's own thoughts in the margins, carrying it around, and memorizing a paragraph here, a paragraph there.

My favorite is a dusty, worn volume of sermons written a hundred years ago by a Methodist preacher. I paid 50 cents for it. Its yellowed pages, some loose, are brittle, torn, and well-marked. Its language is Shakespearean, its passion Pauline, its grandeur and loftiness, Mosaic. I wouldn't trade it for a year's free ride on the information super highway.

C. S. Lewis, in *Surprised by Joy,* identifies the taproots of his life:

I am the product of long corridors, empty sunlit rooms, upstairs indoor silences, attics explored in solitude, distant noises of gurgling cisterns and pipes, and the noise of wind under the tiles. Also, of endless books.[16]

Where in our mad scramble for the latest time-saving device and our passionate embrace of gadgetry will we find another C. S. Lewis? Or are the times too fraught with motion and noise and interruption to allow for the luxury of introspection and deep, quiet thought?

On November 18, 1863, President Abraham Lincoln rode into Gettysburg. The tall, thin man with the sad face walked a block from the railroad station to the home of David Wills, a local attorney. In a small room upstairs, the President polished and practiced the speech he would give in the morning at the dedication of the Gettysburg National Cemetery.

When a crowd of well-wishers gathered below his window, he leaned out and spoke briefly. Then he returned to the small round table where he wrote on a sheet of plain white paper.

The next morning, he went downstairs, mounted a black steed, and led the way to the battlefield and the scene of so much carnage.

The former mayor of Boston, Everett Edwards, a brilliant orator, had been asked to deliver the main address. The President was invited to bring a few words to the widows and families of the dead. Mr. Edwards spoke for two hours.

Following a hymn, President Lincoln went to the brow of the hill and spoke for 135 seconds. The next day, he boarded a train to return to Washington. It was a troubled time; his speech was a failure, or so he thought.

He could not have known that the Gettysburg Address, written on a sheet of plain white paper, lasting slightly more than two minutes, would be remembered and memorized and quoted by generations to come.

How do you account for this man? What forces came together to produce the intellectual and moral giant who sat in that upstairs room at the small round table and crafted a speech for the ages?

Not long ago, I sat in that room and surveyed the simple furnishings — a bed, wash basin, mirror, a pitcher, and some towels. White gloves and black stove pipe hat lay on the bed.

I fixed my eyes on the wax figure of the tall man sitting at the small round table — black trousers, white collarless shirt, white suspenders, black boots — and mused, Who is this man, born in a log cabin in Kentucky and raised on the Illinois frontier?

Scraping along
In a little shack,
With hardly a shirt
To cover his back,
And a prairie wind
To blow him down,
Or pinching the times
If we went to town.[17]

Without radio or television, E-mail or fax machines; without the advantage of hardware and software and Windows and Word Perfect; without benefit of formal schooling and with access to only a few books — the Bible, Shakespeare, *Pilgrim's Progress,* some American and classical history, and Blackstone's commentaries on the law — Lincoln became an extraordinary reader, poring over the pages of his books.

He read and reread those wonderful sentences, copied out long passages and committed them to memory. The disappointments and discipline of those years turned a boy into a man, fashioned a character, forged a leader, and saved a nation.

Where in our noisy, violent, stressful world are we producing an Abraham Lincoln, a C. S. Lewis, a G. K. Chesterton?

SILENCING THE DISTRACTIONS

Today, many Americans are buying bigger and better television screens with enhanced picture and superior sound. Why? So they can see and hear ten-foot dinosaurs swallowing live, screaming human beings — and all within the comfort of their own homes? Or watch in bloody Technicolor as Arnold Schwarzenegger blows away his enemies?

Where in our mad scramble after the latest technology — where in our noisy, violent, stressful world — are we producing an Abraham Lincoln, a C. S. Lewis, a G. K. Chesterton? Will this next generation instead be comprised of Roseannes, Ellens, and Murphy Browns?

The habits developed through years of mindless ease and pleasure have left us — and our children — if not at our worst, very far from our best. Without our permission, television coarsens our sensibility, pidgins our English, and encourages many of us to waste our lives in aimless watching.

With the world tumbling down around us, we would do well to rediscover the interior life — to search out a quiet place at the center. We cannot turn back the clock to a simpler, quieter day, but we must — each in his own way — strive to maintain a quality of life free from the unrelenting, distracting sights and sounds of a decadent age.

Failing to do so will result in a fate far worse than that of a stone-deaf maniac with a broken arm.

CHAPTER FIVE

The "Magic" of Sex Education

The story broke Thursday about mid-afternoon, and confirmation came at six p.m.

Irving "Magic" Johnson appeared on TV to make an announcement that would shock the nation. The three-time winner of the NBA's most valuable player award, who led the Los Angeles Lakers to five world championships, was not smiling when he spoke.

"On November 7, 1991, I retired from professional basketball because a blood test showed I was infected with HIV, the virus that causes AIDS."

The startling news became a hot topic. The talk shows covered the subject with their usual sensation and speculation. The tabloids went even further, leaving no stone unturned to offer up generous helpings of depth and detail, determined not to let the facts stand in the way of a good story. The sound and fury, however, was not always laced with truth.

The truth was bad enough. School counselors and psychologists rushed to the classrooms — the kids must be warned. Sex education with no moral base should occur "early and often."

We were led to believe that if students were given graphic and explicit details of the mechanics of sexuality, AIDS would be eliminated, teen pregnancies would drop, and kids would suddenly — and miraculously — become rational and mature.

The moral confusion of that time was maddening. Anyone searching for common sense is still looking.

Early in his rookie year, the 1979-80 NBA season, Johnson injured his knee. "I was never so scared in my life," he said during an interview. "I started seeing my basketball career going down the drain. I started wondering what I was going to do if it was over. I screamed for my Momma."[1]

That season the Lakers won the title. In the final game, Johnson scored 42 points.

"Magic?" he was asked.

"Yeah," he replied, "I guess the night was magic. . . ."

The sexual revolution was also magic. Disregarding biblical guidelines and ridding themselves of ancient beliefs, a willing and eager clientele bought into the program. This was more than indiscretion in the back seat of a car. It went beyond a secret tryst in the park. This was big-time romance.

Unlike an earlier period when morals mattered, the media got on board, and the churches silently complied. Educators did little to apply the brakes.

What would become a nightmare and national disgrace began as one big party. We could have danced all night.

The result was worse than a skinned knee. The cost in terms of teenage pregnancy, sexually transmitted disease, emotional pain, and economic loss — not to mention the fracture of our cultural base — was enormous.

The result? A crassness, a coarseness, a cheapening of human life — and crying for Momma didn't help.

What would become a nightmare and national disgrace began as one big party. We could have danced all night.

LIFE IN THE FAST LANE

Magic Johnson says he lived life in the fast lane as a superstar and "never was at a loss for female companionship."

It was doubtful he kept pace with Wilt Chamberlain, another basketball star whose biography was released about the time of Johnson's announced resignation. Chamberlain claims to have bedded 20,000 women since the age of 15.

Someone noted that would average 1.2 women per day, which didn't leave much time for church work or the Boy Scouts.

Conduct has consequences. For Magic, the consequences were not good.

Bad news came when Dr. Michael Millman, the team physician, telephoned Magic at his hotel room in Salt Lake City before an exhibition game on October 25 and said, "I need to see you in my office today."

Magic flew back to Los Angeles where Dr. Millman told him he had tested positive for the virus that leads to AIDS.

I questioned long and hard the propriety of including in this book something as personal and tragic as the disclosure that Magic Johnson had tested HIV positive.

Is it proper, I wondered. Is it decent?

When I considered the enormous impact of his life, read the book he wrote, and listened to his public statements and those made about him, I concluded that this was no longer a private matter. It was more than a personal saga.

Magic himself decided to make it public, and in the public domain it has been discussed, analyzed, written about, and has served as the theme of countless talk shows and media pieces. Because of the widespread distribution of inaccurate and damaging information, I felt compelled to pursue it.

Magic Johnson is a role model — and, in many respects, a worthy role model. He has put his life up as one to learn from. Let's face it. Magic is a hero to many — kids and adults alike.

I recently ate at a McDonald's in the Midwest, where the restaurant was decorated in a sports motif. There, along with others, was a life-size portrait of Magic Johnson. Apparently, AIDS has not diminished his appeal.

In his book, *What You Can Do to Avoid AIDS,* Magic seems to have a sincere desire to help kids. The kind of advice the book offers, however, has contributed to our nation's continuing runaway scandal of illegitimate births, broken hearts, and broken homes.

To let such "advice" go unchallenged is no less dangerous than licensing the sale of poisoned food or dispensing inferior airplane parts.

ANYTHING GOES

This chapter may be unpleasant, but much of life is unpleasant. Burying our heads in the sand will not make it any less so. It is no more indelicate to discuss these issues than it is for a surgeon to excise a tumor or amputate a limb. Both procedures are sometimes necessary to save a life.

It is time to take off the rose-colored glasses and acknowledge that we are in a war. This is no backyard barbecue or Sunday school picnic. This is conflict, and the stakes are high.

Do I feel for Magic? Of course, but I also feel for the many faceless women Magic infected. They will die unknown for the thrill of a one-night stand.

This discussion forcefully illustrates the moral insanity of our time. If it is ignorance, we must enlighten. If it is a deliberate attempt to overthrow the moral values we have embraced for centuries, we must resist.

We are in a serious moral conflict, and the stakes are high.

The Bible, the forgotten book, may have a word for it — "willfully ignorant."

Is there not a cause? Is there not a God? Is there no moral dimension? Are there no eternal consequences?

Commenting on an ad that shows a woman resisting sexual advances unless there's protection, *Christianity Today* editorializes:

The penalties are worse than the ad makers realize. The young woman says she is not willing to die for it. Really? Then let the ads also show not only the penalties that *nature* is beginning to exact for immorality in this life, but also the penalties God will impose in the age to come.

The kind of sex education Planned Parenthood provides is "value neutral." In other words — anything goes.

Humanistic sex education, however, does not eliminate improper sexual activity. Every survey shows it *increases* it.

Magic Johnson confesses as much while purporting to "educate" the kids. He writes, "It wasn't so much that I didn't have information about HIV and AIDS. It was right there in my face, on the radio and TV, in newspapers and magazines. The LA Lakers had lectures in the locker room. . . ."[2]

Later he says to students, "I want to give you the education, skills, and support to protect yourself and others — not only against HIV but also against other sexually transmitted diseases and unwanted pregnancy."

There is never a mention, not once, never anything about God or the consequences of sin.

He says, "If you are already sexually active, I know you are probably not going to stop."

How ridiculous. We don't apply that kind of irrationality to anything else in life.

"But you do have a choice," Magic continues. "It's something to consider. However, I realize returning to abstinence isn't always realistic. Be smart enough to be careful."[3]

This kind of talk betrays our children and leads to tragedy.

Magic tells his readers where to get free condoms, suggesting they go to Planned Parenthood offices.

We know that condoms are safe 80 to 85 percent of the time — odds we wouldn't tolerate in any other area of life. We demand precision from the airline pilot, the dentist, meat inspector, pharmacist, mechanic, and banker. We even want our barber to have some idea of what he is doing.

I recently switched banks after the one I had been with ten years twice lost track of my account. I work too hard for my money to tolerate a 20 percent failure rate in those who handle it.

"If someone won't have sex with you without a condom, you are better off letting that person go," Magic advises. "This can be really hard."

Breaking up is hard to do, no doubt about it. But how about this advice: Don't have sex until you're married because that is how our Creator intended — and commands — you to live?

"We can't expect hormonally challenged kids to abstain from sex!" the critics of abstinence education exclaim. "That's much too hard."

You think that is hard. Try giving birth in a school bathroom during the prom! Try having your baby's tiny body sucked out of your womb with a vacuum cleaner! Try going through life knowing you took the life of a child.

That's what I call hard.

Thank God, however, there is forgiveness for any sin through the blood of Jesus Christ. "All have sinned and fall short of the glory of God," but "by faith are you saved."

What we should be telling kids is that it's much easier to live a life pleasing to God — both now and in eternity.

Humanistic sex education does not eliminate improper sexual activity. Every survey shows it *increases* it.

"LIKE IT OR NOT"

Magic addresses parents with these words of advice: "It's not enough to say 'no sex' or 'you can't,' because, like it or not, it's your child who will decide when he or she is ready. You must, therefore, also teach your kids about safer sex."

Really? Why can't parents just say no?

Increasingly intrusive government has entered the tobacco wars, slapping heavy fines on the big companies, curtailing advertising, and prohibiting the sale of cigarettes to children.

Did the government say, "We know you're going to smoke anyway, so use a filter"? Or did they recommend finding a "safer" brand or limiting the number of smokes?

No. They simply said, "Don't do it."

Now merchants are fined for selling to minors, and minors are breaking the law when they purchase and use tobacco.

Let's look at the government's other public service campaigns:

■ "Just say no to drugs." Do the ads tell parents, "We know your kids are going to use drugs — like it or not — just make sure they have clean needles"?

■ "Don't drive under the influence of alcohol." Do they say, "If you are going to drink and drive, be sure to fasten your seat belt"?

What happens when it comes to something as personal and holy as sexual activity? Parents, teachers, and the social planners refuse to advise "Just say no!"

Instead, they say, "Go ahead and do it, just be careful."

We don't apply this ridiculous principle of caution to any other dangerous practice.

A friend of mine recently buried his son who died of AIDS. The young man's agonizing death was absolutely horrible. But there is something worse than dying of AIDS. It is falling into the hands of God without having your sins covered by the blood of Jesus Christ.

Shortly after Johnson's announcement, I happened to be speaking in Springfield, Massachusetts — where the basketball hall of fame is located. One afternoon I went for a visit.

Posters, pictures, memorabilia, clippings, exhibits, jerseys, and sneakers worn by the honorees filled the displays. In the corner of one room a video plays. It features Magic Johnson addressing a circle of kids who had gathered around as he gives pointers on how to improve their game.

I remember something he said: "The coach isn't going to adjust to you — you adjust to the coach."

There was no "like it or not" in that.

In his book, Magic has this advice for his readers, "I think the best thing you can do as a teenager is postpone sexual activity with another person as long as you can."

What else could Magic say? I'm sure his intentions are sincere, but Magic apparently has no moral or religious base from which to advise teens about proper sexual behavior.

Unless the old-fashioned Bible principles of chastity, virginity, and purity are instilled in young people, they have no reason — nor any power — to abstain or even restrain themselves.

A POCKETFUL OF CONDOMS

A brochure recently came in the mail underwritten by a grant from the Henry J. Kaiser family. Journalist and television personality Linda Ellerbee is the honorary chairperson of this organization called Children Now. The brochure, "Talking With Kids About Tough Issues," discusses sexual matters, violence, drugs, gangs, etc.

The word AIDS appears 90 times in this brief brochure, but the word God is not mentioned once. There is no mention of morals. There is no mention of a fixed standard of conduct. No reference to the Bible. It warned about AIDS without noting that the dreaded disease is preventable since it is contracted primarily through unhealthy and unnatural sexual acts.

The most incredible information in this brochure involved a discussion about drug and alcohol abuse. This is the advice it offered:

> Establish a clear family policy on drugs. It's okay to simply say, "We don't allow any drug use, and children in this family are not allowed to drink alcohol."
>
> Teach children to follow rules. Establishing a family policy on drugs will not do any good unless your children already know how to obey rules. That's why it's best to give them practice in compliance by setting up and expecting them to obey rules for everyday situations. . . . Once he knows there is a price to pay, he is more likely to listen when you set firm rules about drugs and alcohol.[4]

Now there's a novel suggestion: Teach children to obey rules! Where did they get that one from? I wonder if Ms. Ellerbee knows that the Bible says, "Children, obey your parents"?

In another section dealing with violence and gangs, the brochure makes this unique recommendation:

> Take a stand. Don't cave into your child's assertion that "everybody else does it.". . . Set firm limits regarding children's actions toward others. Be clear such behavior isn't permitted.[5]

In other words, don't tolerate any behavior that is going to lead to drug and alcohol abuse or violence and gangs.

But when it comes to sexuality, parents are told to back off because, "like it or not," kids are going to do it, and there's nothing we can do about it.

Parents who take that attitude are giving a tacit invitation to young people — whose hormones have already kicked in — to do whatever they feel like doing.

When Boston mayor Ray Flynn ridiculed the notion of the distribution of free condoms and stated it was "something less than a terrific idea," people jumped all over him for it.

One mother, in a letter to the newspaper, sided with Flynn. She wrote:

> Speaking as a mother, Ray Flynn has said exactly the right thing. Quite frankly, the idea of some 15-year-old boy walking around with a pocketful of condoms does not exactly make me

feel more secure about my daughter's future health and well being. When a kid gets a learner's permit to drive, you expect in fairly short order he will want to drive the family car. What do think happens when you hand him a condom?

This mother's common sense, however, is sadly lacking in the "safe sex" propaganda fed to America's children.

NO RESTRICTIONS APPLY

Magic Johnson's announcement almost brought some schools to a standstill.

Hartford, Connecticut's Fox Middle School shifted into something approaching a national emergency: no regular classes, no math, no science.

"We talked about AIDS all day," Ronnell Tyson, age 14, said. "They gave out condoms at school."

He said a sign on the bulletin board read, "If you've been having a lot of sex lately, go see the nurse."

One girl said, "I have been buying my 16-year-old brother condoms for a long time. I don't want him to die."

Magaly Pagan, recreational assistant at Glastonbury High School, said her aunt died of AIDS several years ago after contracting the disease from her uncle. "People are talking about it on the bus," she said. "They are talking about it more seriously than ever."

Dr. Mervyn Silverman, president of the American Foundation For AIDS Research, spouts the liberal line:

The least I would like to see is an expanded and relatively hands-off education program focused on the young — one unencumbered by a conservative agenda. Because of the nature of the audience we are trying to reach, it may have to be explicit.[6]

In other words, we don't want any moral or religious stipulations put on what we can say and show and teach our kids!

Silverman continues, "Nor is it important how he contracted the virus."

Why not?

Whatever happened to waiting to have sex after marriage, or abstinence? As a society, we don't aim high enough anymore.
— Barbara Reynolds

Barbara Reynolds, however, made sense — as she often does. Writing in *USA Today,* she notes:

In preventing pregnancy, condoms have a 14 to 20 percent failure rate. If condoms aren't so hot in preventing life, how did they become perfect

in preventing death? Whatever happened to
waiting to have sex after marriage, or abstinence? As a society, we don't aim high enough
anymore.[7]

For some reason educators and the media consider
the idea of "waiting until marriage" to be passé and
politically incorrect. The *New York Times* called Dan
Quayle's forthright position for abstinence a "blind
spot," as if self-denial and self-discipline were some
kind of anomaly.

When it comes to "safe sex," no restrictions apply.

THE DEATH THREAT

Anna Quindlen's rhapsody takes the cake. In a
New York Times column titled, "Believe in Magic,"
she writes:

Some basketball players, because of their height
and certain hauteur, seem to demand genuflec-
tion. Magic Johnson always looks to me like a
guy you should hug. That was especially true
when he told the world he was infected with
the AIDS virus, and said he was going to become a national spokesman, and flashed the
grin nonetheless. What a man![8]

What about the infected women Magic left behind?
Many will be shunned because of this illness and die

without the adulation heaped on the famous basketball star.

Anna Quindlen continues, illustrating the complete moral and intellectual bankruptcy that characterizes the blind leaders of our lost nation:

We obsess about "lifestyle" in the midst of a pyramid scheme of mortality and infectious disease spreading exponentially.

I don't want to hear anymore about how condoms shouldn't be advertised on television and in the newspapers. I don't want to hear anymore about the impropriety of clean needle exchanges or the immorality of AIDS education is schools.

On Thursday night, our eight-year-old asked about safe sex after he heard those words from Magic Johnson's mouth. And I was amazed at how simple and straightforwardly I was able to discuss it.

I don't want to hear anymore about good people who aren't going to live to be 40, about wasted talent and missed chances, or about children who die before their fathers and mothers do. I'm far less concerned about my kids' lifestyles than I am about their lives.[9]

Ms. Quindlen doesn't get it! The correlation between lifestyle and life is one of life and death.

The inability to understand this correlation betrays the abysmal ignorance that is the birthright of unbelief. When the truth of God's Word is forsaken, rational thinking becomes impaired, common sense takes flight, and one is left to his own devices. Nothing remains as an absolute. Everyone does what is right in his own eyes.

The final sentence in Quindlen's article illustrates the confusion, "Will this finally make them [parents] say to their kids, 'It could happen to you,' finally making them stop relying solely on chastity and start dealing with reality?"

In other words, chastity is too hard so we will threaten them with reality — death by AIDS.

FUN, SAFE SEX

Dr. James Dobson of Focus on the Family was invited by Secretary Otis Bowen of the Department of Health and Human Services to serve on a commission dealing with teenage pregnancy. After agreeing to the assignment, Dr. Dobson was appointed to the teen pregnancy prevention panel.

Early in the panel's first meeting, when Dr. Dobson made reference to abstinence, he noticed most of the other members "blanched, then began sweating, trembling and gasping for air."

When he discovered that 15 of the 18 panel members wanted to teach kids how to have lots of "really fun, safe sex," he and two others called a press conference and resigned from the commission.

A number of years ago, the philosophy of "fun, safe sex" would have been absolutely rejected by all but the porno merchants and the loyal savants of Margaret Sanger.

Dobson said, "Under these circumstances, what hope is there that the Judeo-Christian system of thought can survive? How can it withstand the daily hammering it takes in the press, from television, from the liberal universities, from People for the American Way, from the ACLU, the National Organization For Women, the National Abortion Rights Action League, and from regular tampering by ambitious and tax obsessed congressmen?"[10]

Dobson quotes James Hitchcock to show that the aim of the humanists is to cause young people to reject the moral traditions that have always undergirded our society:

> Certain proponents of the sexual revolution know exactly what they are doing when they promote it, for they realize that if people of traditional values can be made to change their minds (not even necessarily their behavior) on this matter, they will prove easily malleable in other areas as well. The assault on traditional Christian sexual morality is an attempt to shatter all deeply held, uncompromisable moral convictions to make people into perfectly mobile, infinitely manipulable creatures.[11]

Mary Calderone admits a similar point. As a leader of the modern sex education movement, she says, "If man, as he is, is obsolescent, then what kind do we want to produce in his place, and how do we design the production line? That is the real question facing . . . sex education."

Dobson says this is a surprisingly frank expression of sexual humanistic intentions.

Calderone continues, "Human beings of the brave new world will be 'consciously engineered' by society's best minds, who will provide for the necessary conditioning."[12]

In other words, "Aim for the children!" How many parents want their children to be redesigned for the production line?

HOW-TO SEX TEXTS

While in Pennsylvania recently, I talked with a father who told me, "My fourth-grade daughter forgot a book at home, so I took it to her at school. The classroom was empty, but I found her class in the gym. Guess what they were doing."

Knowing some of what goes on in public schools these days, I cringed.

"These ten-year-olds were being given an explicit lesson on the practice of homosexuality!" the father said.

He was shocked — not only at the graphic nature of the material but the fact that sex education in public schools takes place without any moral instruction on what is right or wrong.

Many parents don't realize that from first grade on, school children are taught that homosexuality is an appropriate alternate lifestyle. They are also taught that abstinence is an "appropriate alternative" rather than the right thing to do.

Sex education in public schools takes place without any moral instruction on what is right or wrong.

One textbook used in some public schools is called *Boys and Sex* by Wardell B. Pomeroy. There are few sentences that I would even dare quote. This "how-to" book on sex shows how a boy can progress from one activity to another.

Pomeroy writes, "Some girls may draw the line at one point or another in the progression I've described, but most people engage in all of this behavior before marriage."

Finally, he states, "Consequently, petting is fun . . . for both boys and girls."[13]

In the companion book, *Girls and Sex,* Pomeroy lists "reasons why a girl might think favorably about having intercourse for the first time." Then he makes this unbelievable statement, "There are many girls who regret after marriage that they didn't have premarital sexual intercourse."[14]

In other words, even the girls who refrain from having sex before marriage are sorry they didn't. At least that's the message these sex educators are trying to get across.

These books, published by Delacorte Press, a division of Bantam Books, are widely used in public schools.

REALITY BASED?

Columnist Cal Thomas explains the downward spiral on which our nation is sliding:

> Jumbo jets full of societal viruses are stacked up over our nation. As each one lands, it unleashes a new outrage, a new strain of depravity. Down and down we go and where we will stop, no one knows.
>
> First it was promiscuity among heterosexuals, a loosening of marital bonds and cohabitation. Next it was the "gay rights" movement, which rhetorically bludgeoned many into silence. Now comes the bisexuals and who's next? Those who practice bestiality or man/boy love?
>
> More important, on what basis can we now tell people that what they practice and believe is bad or wrong? If standards of measurement are tossed out, how can we know if we are getting a true pound?[15]

Patrick Sandovel, writing in the *Denver Post*, ridicules the "abstinence only" position taken by Focus on the Family spokesperson Amy Stephens, whom Sandovel refers to as ultraconservative and far-right. He says:

> Age-appropriate, reality based sexuality education, where properly implemented, has been shown to encourage responsible behavior among teens — especially when young people receive education prior to initiating intercourse.[16]

Mr. Sandovel's statement is absolutely false. In fact, "reality based" teaching simply encourages sexual activity. Every survey shows that the more sex education in a school, the more sexual activity is practiced.

In the three years since the high school in Commerce City, Colorado became one of the first in the nation to hand out condoms, the pregnancy rate among students has soared. In fact, it is 31 percent above the national average of 58.1 births per 1,000 students.[17]

Still, most liberal educators, like Mr. Sandovel, reject the idea of abstinence for teens:

> Abstinence is 100 percent . . . but vows of abstinence break more often than condoms do. According to the Federal Centers For Disease

Control, less than 50 percent of teens abstain from sexual activity. . . . There was never a time when such censorship and distortion of the truth would be accepted as responsible education. In the age of AIDS, it's a deadly form of child abuse.[18]

Once again the idea of calling for abstinence is considered unrealistic and labeled "child abuse." Why? Because to teach abstinence and monogamy requires belief in a moral standard. Could it be that some educators have no moral beliefs; or if they do, are they afraid of being the biggest hypocrites of all?

Every survey shows that the more sex education in a school, the more sexual activity is practiced.

THE SECRET OF SUCCESS

In 1934, after J. D. Unwin studied 86 different societies, the findings were published in his book, *Sex and Culture*. Many scholars — above all, Unwin himself — were startled.

What was the amazing conclusion? That all 86 societies demonstrated a direct tie between monogamy and "expansive energy" of civilization.

Unwin, who had no Christian convictions and applied no moral judgments, wrote, "I offer no opinion about rightness or wrongness." Nevertheless, he had to conclude:

> In human records, there is no instance of a society retaining its energy after a complete new generation has inherited a tradition which does not insist on prenuptial and postnuptial continence.[19]

In this amazing discovery, Unwin found no exceptions to the fact that those societies in which sexual fidelity was valued inevitably flourished.

American educators, however, have taken our children in the opposite direction, and the results are now having a negative impact on society as a whole.

John Silber, president of Boston University, explains why this happened:

> Our society reacted to the sexual revolution with such incompetence that we now have an involuntary enslavement of young Americans at a time in life when they are so immature that they lack the knowledge and the insight to protect themselves. Most societies recorded by anthropologists recognize the fundamental need to regulate and formalize the expression of the sexual instinct.
>
> Sexuality has been recognized a national sacrament in every society that has had any kind of social structure.[20]

A generation ago, C. S. Lewis described in his book, *That Hideous Strength,* the first step in the ultimate "abolition of man." What happens when man's moral nature is eradicated? A deconstructioning process takes place that consists of "the stifling of all deep-seated repugnances."

In other words, when all restraints are removed, man becomes an animal.

Sex education without a moral base can lead our nation — and its citizens — to only one destination: total depravity.

Is that the future you want for your children?

CHAPTER SIX

America's Saddest Day

On a day in 1852 — perhaps the saddest day in America's history — the sons of the Puritans gathered up their children and delivered them into the hands of the state. After years of resistance from its citizens, Massachusetts passed the Compulsory School Attendance Law — the first of its kind in the United States.

From the founding of Massachusetts Bay in 1630, the Puritans had considered the school a vital complement to the local church. Every church member was expected to be educated in order to maintain "doctrinal purity" through study of the Bible.

All was well until 1684. The Massachusetts Bay Colony charter was revoked, and the church's domination of education was threatened by the enactment of the public school law. The people, however, resisted, preferring instead to send their children to private schools.

Samuel L. Blumenfeld's book, *Is Public Education Necessary?*, chronicles the progression from church-maintained schools to publicly funded education. In her review of Blumenfeld's book, Jane Engaham provides this synopsis:

> Towns found ways to get around the law. By 1720, Boston had far more private schools than public, and many towns in Massachusetts no longer had common public schools at all. Every conceivable combination of parental and church instruction — tutorial, apprenticeship, and self-education — sprang up making for great educational freedom and diversity.[1]

For the next almost 130 years, the education of Massachusetts' children remained under local control. The younger children learned to read and write at home, and many parents avoided sending their children to "common schools."

The state of Massachusetts finally realized that unless attendance was made compulsory, public education would cease to exist. In fact, as late as 1820, only 22 percent of Boston's school-age population were enrolled in public schools. But that was soon to change.

THE FINEST MINDS OF ALL TIME

Why the sudden push for government-run schools? Was it because our young nation had neglected to train its children?

In my book, *Come Home America,* I recount the story of how fathers instructed their sons and mothers their daughters — how the church instilled values and the community took the poor under its wings and taught them to read and write.

Without benefit of government mandates, bulging bureaucracies, and truant officers, America produced some of the greatest men and women in history and honed some of the finest minds of all time: George Washington, John and Samuel Adams, Thomas Jefferson, James Madison, James Monroe, George Mason, Patrick Henry, Benjamin Rush, Roger Sherman, Benjamin Franklin — to name a few.

In fact, it was the yearning for freedom from government control that led to the Declaration of Independence and the Revolutionary War. Where was that love of freedom fostered? At the massive regional high school or the sprawling, multi-cultured university campus? No.

Of the 117 men who signed the Declaration of Independence, the Articles of Confederation, and the Constitution, only one out of four had gone to college. George Washington was educated by his father, Benjamin Franklin by his father and a private school, and Thomas Jefferson by a tutor.[2]

Today with our best technology, professional personnel, enormous budgets, and magnificent facilities, America's schools are not coming close to replicating the quality of leadership produced in our nation's early years.

Before the institution of government schooling in the mid-1800s, 90 percent of young people were being educated in some way, and America had a 90 percent literacy rate. How was such remarkable educational success achieved? With home schooling and schools run by the communities and by the churches. The results prove they did a pretty good job!

RADICALLY LITERATE

We didn't discard the humble school in the home or church for the mammoth government system because the teachers were failing. Quite the contrary, as Al Janney, president of the American Association of Christian Schools, explains:

> Between 1600 and 1776, our nation existed without boards of education, federally subsidized schools, teacher training colleges, and federal judges to tell us how to educate children. During that time our nation produced a

generation of people who wrote the Constitution, the best document ever framed for a nation: they desired freedom, decided against the greatest empires in the world, and forged out a nation. They built one of the greatest societies ever known to man, that produced the greatest good to the greatest number of people at the least cost — simply because families and churches decided that their children would have a godly education.[3]

What was the basis of this godly education?

During America's first 150 years, every school child studied from *The New England Primer*, which presented practical advice and Bible truths in rhythmic form for easy memorization. Examples of these aphorisms include:

- Adam and Eve their God did grieve.
- Life to mend this book attend.
- The cat doth play and later slay.
- A dog will bite a thief at night.
- The idle fool is whipped at school.
- Wrought by hand great works to stand.
- Job felt the rod yet blessed his God.
- Queens and kings must lie in the dust.
- Time cuts down all, the great and small.

In addition to *The New England Primer*, over five million copies of Noah Webster's spelling book were purchased by private American citizens. In a country of under 20 million people, that was almost one per household!

In the ten years between 1813 and 1823, Sir Walter Scott's novels sold five million copies in the United States — an amount equal to about 60 million books today! James Fenimore Cooper's books, including *The Last of the Mohicans,* also sold in the millions.

**Compared to modern standards,
our ancestors must have been
radically literate.**

These bestsellers were not light reading. Pick up a Cooper or a Scott at your local library, and you will discover complex, highly allusive prose that would challenge any college student today.

According to the American Library Association, only one adult in eleven today purchases books for personal edification and education. Compared to modern standards, our ancestors must have been radically literate.

AS THEY SAW FIT

In 1812, Pierre DuPont deNemours published *Education in the United States,* a book chronicling America's phenomenally high rate of literacy. "Forty years before passage of the compulsory school laws," DuPont noted that "fewer than four out of every thousand people in the new nation could not read and do numbers well."[4]

DuPont was also amazed that nearly every child was skilled in "argumentation" — the old-fashioned term for critical thinking. He attributed this to the widespread habit of involving young children in disputes about the meaning of difficult Bible passages.

Historically, schooling was about literacy, and that is why it succeeded. Literacy isn't difficult to achieve when children perceive that adults think reading is important.

Before 1852, when Massachusetts passed compulsory schooling, the American people were educating themselves quite well. Some families used traditional schooling while others improvised and employed the resources they had on hand. These early entrepreneurial forms of instruction provided creative and useful ways for children to learn how to read, write, and think. They substituted for formal schooling, as Benjamin Franklin did, "as they best saw fit."

"As they best saw fit" meant the prescription for a free country, and "as the authorities see fit" was considered the formula for dictatorship.

Former New York State Teacher of the Year, John Taylor Gatto, author of *Dumbing Us Down: The Exhausted School* and *The Empty Child,* asks some profound questions and makes a startling conclusion about America's educational system:

We had a perfectly literate country before the advent of government schooling in 1852. What on earth has happened since? Why aren't we as literate in our present well-schooled era as we once were in a lightly schooled one? A look at the course 20th-century schooling has deliberately taken will make it clear we are not in the presence of a simple mistake in social engineering. What has happened was meant to happen.[5]

Can it be that the decline in America's literacy rate was actually programmed by social engineers?

THE TAKEOVER

What happened? Who instituted the diabolical takeover of home-church-community education?

A class of people — who thought they knew better than their fathers — made a conscious decision to move this country down a different road. To do so, they first had to mold and fashion a new breed of people.

Failing to convince the older generation of their lofty aims, they targeted the children. It would be easier that way. After all, as Horace Mann had said, "Men are cast-iron, but children are wax."

As one who despised the cross of Christ and denied the gospel's new birth, Mann's goal was to tear New England's children away from their home-based biblical education and their Puritan heritage.

Although Massachusetts' 1852 compulsory atten-dance law met with stiff opposition in some quarters, the idea of government control of education seemed harmless enough. Within a few years, the other states had adopted similar legislation.

No one could have foreseen the destructive impact government would have when it usurped the role of schoolmaster. The legislators should have listened to James Madison who warned that the government might attempt to "take into their hands the public education of children."

Madison went on to say that if Congress passed laws leading to government-controlled education, "it would subvert the very foundations, and transmute the very nature of the limited government established by the people of America."[6]

In other words, when the government controls the school, freedom is jeopardized. We have only to look at Hitler's Germany and the communism of China and the Soviet Union to realize the truth of Madi-son's statement.

Who disregarded Madison's warning and dreamed up this mandatory attendance law? Horace Mann, the Unitarian who didn't trust parents to teach and train their own children.

REASON NOT REVELATION

On a recent trip to Boston, I walked up Tremont Avenue to the old Park Street Church. Nearby, a sacred cemetery dating back to about 1660 holds the family remains of Benjamin Franklin as well as Paul Revere, John Hancock, Samuel Adams, and victims of the Boston Massacre. A block away, the Boston State House sits proudly across the street from the oldest park in America, the Boston Common.

Touring the magnificent capitol building with its impressive rotunda and marble hallways, I admired the pictures and framed speeches on the walls, the tapestries, statues, and memorabilia. On my way out, a sculpture caught my eye. Perched on a pedestal by a side door, it depicted two hands holding the world. A bronze marker identified the artfully crafted object simply: Creation.

In the beginning God created the heavens and the earth. This is my Father's world. He made it. And He made us.

These thoughts washed over my soul as I stepped outside to be greeted by a larger-than-life statue of the "father of public education" — the Unitarian Horace Mann. Abruptly, I was reminded of the age-long war between good and evil — God, the Creator, and man, the fallen creature. The fallen creature would usurp the place of God and, employing children as pawns, create his own world without divine intervention.

The pieces of the puzzle came together when I walked up another block and discovered the head-quarters of the Unitarian Church. A brochure outlines their tenets of faith:

Unitarian Universalism has differed from mainline Western and Eastern faiths by claiming that truth is multifaceted and elusive. Whereas there may be many different truths in our lives, The Truth is not accessible to human grasp.

Unitarian-Universalist minister Greta Crosby declares, "I want to tell the truth, the whole truth and nothing but the truth, but The Truth is not simple but complex."

The brochure further states, "You will find no single pathway to God or enlightenment, instead there are numerous worthy routes that have been demonstrated by Unitarian-Universalists throughout history."

In 1819, well-known clergyman William Ellery Channing delivered "The Baltimore Sermon" in which he claimed "reason" rather than revelation as the instrumental source of his faith. That sermon, in effect, launched the Unitarian controversy and denomination.

As we have seen before, the results were far-reaching. When unbelief flourishes in the pulpits, it taints everything it touches. Such was the case in 1819.

What do Unitarians believe? Or, more correctly, what do they not believe? They reject the Bible as the inspired Word of God and do not consider Jesus to be the Son of God. They deny the doctrine of the Trinity — one God in three persons.

The brochure continues, "Furthermore, we come to our religious values experientially. The beliefs we hold are not so much revealed to us as experienced by us."

With that statement in mind, it is not hard to understand their philosophy of education: "We encourage our children to develop their own working wisdoms instead of inheriting the truths of their parents or tradition."

Unlike the Puritans who considered it their godly mandate to pass on the truths of God's Word to their children, the Unitarians encourage their offspring to make up their own version of wisdom and truth.

**When unbelief flourishes in the pulpits,
it taints everything it touches.**

HOW TO CONTROL A NATION

Along with other elitists, Horace Mann determined to change the direction of America. Knowing he could not "improve" society through legislation or by working through adults, he hit on a new idea: Aim for the children.

In 1837, he wrote to a friend explaining his new strategy:

I have abandoned jurisprudence, and betaken myself to the larger sphere of mind and morals, having found the present generation composed of materials almost unmalleable, I'm about transferring my efforts to the next. Men are cast iron but children are wax.[7]

Opposed to Orthodox Christianity, Horace Mann saw the public schools as "a means for the state to control people."

Newton Bateman, a late 19th century advocate of public education, echoed Mann's sentiments, claiming:

Government has a right of eminent domain over the minds, souls, and bodies of us all. Therefore, education cannot be left to the caprices and contingencies of individuals.[8]

Why this urge to dominate the free people of America? The answers come from a European nation well-known in modern times for its propensity for deception.

Although compulsory school attendance was Horace Mann's dream child, it was also the fulfillment of German philosopher Georg Friedrich Hegel's (1770-1831) plan for the future. Hegel's critics had warned that Hegelianism was "so devoutly godless . . . that it may call for the destruction of the world."

What was this godless philosophy? That the state is supreme and that people are pawns who must be subordinated to the government.

In fact, history records that Hegel's philosophy contributed to the bloodshed of two world wars — both of which involved military aggression precipitated by a statist obsession with world domination.

And there you have it. The philosophy that sparked Leninism, Nazism, socialism, communism, Maoism. And how did these efforts accomplish their goals? By establishing government controlled schools.

THE PRUSSIAN MODEL

Few Americans realize that the structure of 20th-century American schooling is modeled on a system invented in early 19th-century Prussia.

After Napoleon's amateur army beat Prussia's professional soldiers at the battle of Jena in 1806, Prussia's leaders began searching for answers to their military dilemma. The search ended with philosopher Johann Fichte, who in his famous "address to the German people," presented a new course for the nation. The goal? To re-shape the educational system and create a nation in which everyone would learn how to take orders.

"Modern 'forced' schooling," as John Gatto explains, "began in Prussia with a clear vision of what a centralized educational system could deliver":

- Obedient soldiers for the army
- Obedient workers for the mines
- Subservient civil servants for the government

- Subservient clerks for industry
- Citizens who thought alike about major issues[9]

How did educators hope to achieve such docile, submissive, and brainwashed citizens? By keeping them illiterate. The ultimate goal of the Prussian system was to unify the citizenry under a centralized leadership.

According to John Gatto's research, a small number of American ideological leaders, including Horace Mann of Massachusetts, Calvin Stowe of Ohio, Barnus Sears of Connecticut, and others, visited Prussia in the first half of the 19th century. Awed by the "order, obedience, and efficiency" of Prussian society, the visitors attributed the nation's success to its educational system. Upon returning to America, these men were determined to bring the Prussian model to our new nation.

What had impressed them? Gatto explains:

The Prussians had everything the reformers wanted — uniform curriculum through state controlled texts, compulsory attendance, full financial support via taxation, truant officers, graded classrooms, and teachers trained by the state.[10]

Sound familiar? You probably didn't know that modern-day America's public school system is an exact replica of 19th-century, government-controlled Prussian education.

PREPARED TO TAKE ORDERS

About this time, Utopian socialist colonies were springing up across the United States. These colonies provided a testing ground for the Prussian model of an idyllic childhood — one free of care and responsibility.

Why the need for children raised in a carefree environment? Because it was easier to apply "behavior modification techniques to children who knew very little and were only modestly literate, than it was to shape people who had been trained early in thinking techniques."[11]

In other words, the more uneducated the child the more moldable his behavior — and the better prepared for a lifetime of taking orders.

Clarence B. Carson, in *A Basic History of the United States*, explains that the goal of "the public school movement" was not to provide "free" schooling for all of America's children so the nation could have an educated, informed citizenry. "It was aimed at the children," Carson writes, "impinged upon the family, and entailed the use of government power in ways which endangered . . . the life, liberty, and property of Americans."[12]

The push for centralized, government-controlled schools had — from the beginning and continues today — one objective in mind: To round up America's children and corral them into state-run behavior modification centers.

Carson's research brought him to this conclusion:

The most zealous of the reformers were determined to use the power of the state by way of
the schools to break the hold of religious tradition and inherited culture, and to change society through the child's training.[13]

Nothing has changed. The goal of liberal educators
remains the same today. It is nothing less than the
total transformation of society, with children the
conduit through whom socialism is achieved.

**Centralized, government-controlled
schools had . . . one objective in mind:
To round up [our] children and corral them
into state-run behavior modification centers.**

FORCED PUBLIC SCHOOLING

By 1852, educators began their first efforts to force
public school attendance on the American people.
Why? Because children had to be separated from
parental, cultural, and religious influences and
isolated in a learning environment where they could
be molded into compliant citizens.

Under the leadership of Horace Mann and others,
one state after another adopted the Prussian method

of schooling and imposed it upon America's communities.

Clarence Carson notes the ultimate consequences of this decision:

> Horace Mann's law permanently altered the course of American education in the Prussian direction, taking educational policy out of local hands and putting it in the hands of a state educational bureaucracy.[14]

For more than 100 years, the one-room schoolhouse had stood as the common man's symbol of hope for their children's future. In nearly every settlement and town, pioneer farmers, ranchers, pastors, and tradesmen had joined forces to provide teachers and books for their children's education.

John Gatto explains that these community schools were "highly effective as an academic transmitter, breeders of self-reliance and independence in their young students, intimately related to their communities . . . and largely unadministrated."[15]

It was the success of these small locally-controlled schools that made them a threat to the new educational experiment — and eventually led to the demise of the little red schoolhouse. Why? Because academic achievement and independent thinking were no longer the purpose of education. The goal had become one of absolute control.

Now you know why today most neighborhood schools are a thing of the past and why children are transported to huge, consolidated centers miles from home.

WHEN READING IS DANGEROUS

By the end of the last century, the stage had been set for Act One. The script had been written and the players assigned their parts for participation in the coming "collective society." No independent, self-reliant thinkers need apply.

What posed the greatest danger to this new plan for America? Literacy. In his own words, humanist educator John Dewey described why reading is dangerous:

> In modern society, people would be defined by their associations, the groups to which they belonged, not by their own individual accomplishments. In such a world, people who read too well or too early are dangerous because they know how to find out what they don't know all by themselves without consulting experts.[16]

In an effort to eliminate people who could read "too well or too early," Dewey advocated abandoning the "phonics" method of teaching reading. Why? Because students who learned to read phonetically were able to master any word by simply "sounding it out." With the "look-say" method, which Dewey espoused, students learned to read only those words taught them by their instructors.

Why did Dewey seek to abandon the successful phonetic method of reading instruction? Because the ability to read challenging, mind-expanding material produces thinkers who can't be easily "socialized" — or controlled. And that's the last thing humanist educators wanted.

Somewhere around the turn of the century, "making people dumb for their own good" became the goal behind enforced schooling.

DUMB FOR THEIR OWN GOOD

Somewhere around the turn of the century, "making people dumb for their own good" became the goal behind enforced schooling.

In the book, *Government Nannies: The Cradle to Grave Agenda of Goals 2000 and Outcome Based Education,* John Taylor Gatto explains the powerful forces motivating this movement:

I know you will find this hard to believe, yet the track of the Prussianization of America over the past 150 years is quite clear. Beginning in the late 19th century and continuing through today, a small band of very influential people, substantially financed by money provided by the large private foundations like Carnegie, Rockefeller, and Ford, have introduced what might be called "modified scientific socialism" into American institutional education.[17]

How were the goals of these "influential people" accomplished? By gaining control of the "machinery of government," they "began to destroy the mechanism of local control of schools," Gatto writes. To avoid public criticism of their sinister efforts, these powerful men also gained "control of the public oversight mechanisms of journalism, which provided a cloak of invisibility over what was happening."

This small band of influential people had determined privately that this was the best course for the American state, and so with no public discussion and little wasted motion, they pointed our nation down the statist road. We were going to become a multi-tiered class society like Germany or Japan, and that is in fact what we are well on our way to becoming.[18]

And who lands at the bottom of the tier? You and me, our children and our grandchildren.

The elitist manipulators are dismissive of most Americans — especially evangelical, Bible-believing Christians. We're well on our way toward Aldous

Huxley's *Brave New World*, and Donna Shalala's "seamless system of interventions from prenatal care through the early grades." This may be our last wake-up call.

CHAPTER SEVEN

Conflict in the Classroom

John Dunphy said in *The Humanist,* January 1983, "I'm convinced that the battle for humankind's future must be waged and won in the public school classrooms by teachers."[1]

What kind of teachers? Those "who correctly perceive their role as the proselytizers of a new faith, a religion of humanity that recognizes and respects the spark of what theologians call divinity in every human being," according to humanist Dunphy.

What plans do humanist educators have for the public school classroom? "The classroom must and will become an arena of conflict between the old and the new."

What do humanists consider the old? The "rotting corpse of Christianity together with all its adjacent evils and misery."

How do they define "the new"? As the "new faith
of humanism, resplendent in its promise of a world
in which the never realized Christian ideal of 'love
thy neighbor' will finally be achieved."

**The new faith of humanism, with teachers
as its proselytizers, will attempt to replace
"the rotting corpse of Christianity."**

MAN'S GREATEST DISCOVERY

Education, mandated and enforced by the states,
was supposed to bring out the best in students and
pave the way for utopia in our time. The common
school, Horace Mann wrote, "is the greatest discovery ever made by man."

Why such a bold statement? Because Mann knew
the power behind the public school, where America's
children could be molded and brainwashed without
the interference of wise and loving parents.

According to Mann, society would be much improved by the "common school":

Let the common school be expanded to its capa-
bilities, let it be worked with the efficiency of
which it is susceptible, and nine-tenths of the
crimes in the penal code would become obso-
lete; the long catalogue of human ills would be

abridged; men would walk more safely by day; every pillow would be more inviolable by night; property, life, and character held by a stronger tenure; all rational hopes respecting the future brightened.[2]

The bright future Mann described has yet — after almost 150 years of public education — to materialize. In fact, crime and "human ills" have increased dramatically to the point where in some cities people are afraid to walk the streets in broad daylight! John Silber said:

Our society is in trouble and we all know it. We know that something is terribly wrong — the way we might know in our bodies that we are seriously ill. When we have an internal intimation that we have a serious illness, it is hard to even talk about the way we feel. We sense that talking about it might make it worse, but we compare the way we feel now with the way we used to feel. In other words, we say, "I didn't used to have this queasiness. It didn't hurt when I bent *that* way. My coffee doesn't taste right anymore. Sometimes life doesn't seem like worth the fight, but I don't feel like quitting either."[3]

Most of us know these symptoms, but today it isn't ourselves but our country that we worry about.

We sense something is wrong, but we don't know what to do about it.

What symptoms tell us our society is ill? The failure of our public education system is one.

At one time, our one-room schools — even in unpromising backwoods environments — were capable of producing not only an Abraham Lincoln but a well-educated, literate population fully capable of following the Lincoln-Douglas debates. Now the schools turn out millions of functionally "ill"-literate graduates, effectively deprived any cultural heritage.

Now the schools turn out millions of functionally "ill"-literate graduates, effectively deprived any cultural heritage.

A SYSTEM GONE AWRY

In his book, *Have the Public Schools "Had It"?*, Elmer Towns traces the origin and development of public education — from the earliest days when the home, church, and community trained their young to the present when the government controls the schools.

Fairly and objectively, Dr. Towns weighs the strengths of the two methods against their weaknesses. He enumerates the positive achievements and applauds the teachers for their efforts but worries about the effects of a system gone awry.

Towns, a former college president and lifelong educator, does not advocate abandonment of the public schools. He does not make reckless charges or dredge up the most extreme examples of dereliction; but he is troubled by what he sees.

Since Dr. Towns wrote his book a quarter of a century ago, much has changed. If he was troubled then, what would he say now?

Julius Becton offers a first-hand assessment of the government school. Becton, a combat veteran of World War II, Korea, and Vietnam, was given the assignment of reforming — what some call — "the worst school system in America." This 70-year-old battle-scarred, retired, three-star general, who currently oversees the Washington, D.C. schools, calls the assignment "the toughest job I've ever had."

A Washington D.C. grade school teacher reports that many of the fifth and sixth grade students in her geography class were unable to locate their hometown — the nation's capital — on a map of the United States.

Washington's schools may unfairly represent the nation's education establishment, but throw a heavy dose of welfarism into the mix, and they illustrate what happens when parents surrender their children to the state.

"The cities have been murdered by their schools," declared Jerrold R. Zacharias, professor of physics at the Massachusetts Institute of Technology and pioneer in education innovation. "If the schools were good, we could handle the other problems."[4]

In other words, if schools were teaching values and providing kids with an education that would prepare them for college and/or the workplace, many of our social problems — gangs, unemployment, welfare — would be solved.

"YOU CAN'T TOUCH ME!"

Is public education on its last leg? R. W. Seltzer thinks so. In an article titled, "Public Education: Is Its Demise Near?", published in *The Clearing House* magazine, he writes, "At the present rate of deterioration, public education as it exists today will be dead by the year 2000."

Barring swift and decisive corrective action, government education has "had it." How do we know? Destruction is inevitable whenever the desire to be politically correct replaces a passion for unswerving moral certainty.

Our public school system encourages rebellion and defiance of authority.

William Waugh, the Associated Press education writer, warned: "America's high schools — from the ghetto to the suburbs — are like boiling cauldrons. No one can predict when the pot will boil over, but already violence, vandalism, and noisy protests are common."[5]

Mr. Waugh goes on to describe schools that "operate in a prison-like atmosphere — armed guards, fenced school yards, and locked classrooms."

"Teachers are in a constant state of fear," according to Lee Dolson, president of the San Francisco Classroom Teachers' Association. He claims teachers want help "even if it takes police patrolling the halls of every school."[6]

Could it be that the problems facing the public school systems go beyond academics?

Elmer Towns lays it on the line:

Our students have been told to express themselves — they do. Our students have been told to demand their rights — they do. Our students have been told to defy injustice — they do. But their self-esteem is outside the law. Their demands are without rational basis. Their defiance of injustice is aimed at the wrong cause, because that which they defy is not injustice, but their personal prejudice.[7]

No wonder America's schools are in such chaos. The system itself has encouraged rebellion and defiance of authority. As a result, the inmates are running the asylum.

Teachers and administrators are powerless to regain control. Why? Because to do so educators must deny the very philosophy of "freedom" they have been espousing to their students for years.

Dr. Towns agrees:

The case against the public schools reeks like their dirty restrooms. Some literature books read like the bathroom walls. Young "latrine lawyers" sneer at education. "You can't touch me," they say, and defy discipline.[8]

How long can public schools survive when they fail to understand that their role is to teach and impart knowledge, not to serve as babysitters or therapists bent on remaking society?

WE WANT YOUR CHILDREN

Former Tennessee governor Lamar Alexander — who later served as secretary of education — speaking at the 1991 Governors' Conference of Education in Wichita, Kansas, said he envisions a "brand-new American school" open year round from six a.m. to six p.m.

Washington bureaucrats want parents to surrender . . . their toddlers to this failed experiment in mind control.

Remember, this is the same American school system that needs armed guards to protect students from killing one another — and the teachers. Now Washington bureaucrats want parents to surrender not only their kindergartners but their toddlers to this failed experiment in mind control.

Take note of Lamar Alexander's plan for your children in the "new America school":

These schools will serve from age three months to age 18. That may be a shocking thought to you, but if you were to do an inventory of every baby in your community, and think about what the needs of those babies were for the next four or five years, you might see that those needs might not be served any other way.[9]

Is he saying that no one can meet the needs of infants and children except government-run institutional day care from infancy to adulthood? Haven't we had enough government interference within our families? Must Big Brother oversee the education — and parenting — of our children?

Donna Shalala, Clinton's Secretary of Health and Human Services, says that "serving younger children ties in with the Administration's goal of creating a 'seamless' system of interventions from prenatal care through the early grades."[10]

In other words, "We want your children." That sounds like an excerpt from an old Soviet textbook.

What has been sacrificed to reach the goals of this "seamless" system? Truth. In fact, the repudiation of objective truth is visible at all levels of public education.

In Tacoma, Washington, an exam was given to grammar school students who were asked to circle one of three possible answers and give a reason for his choice. Each of the answers was acceptable, no one more "correct" than the other. The stated purpose of the test was to show that "there are few things in life that have one correct answer."[11]

In other words, "Kids, you have to judge for yourself what is right and what is wrong. If it feels right, do it. You are your own little god. Go to it. Let the chips fall where they may. Just be yourself. No boundaries."

Translate that to the government, and you have New Jersey's governor Christine Todd Whitman who said, "When it comes to social issues, I'm not all one way or the other."

AT ITS LOWEST LEVEL

The lack of sound educational policies in America's public schools has left a tragic legacy of educational mediocrity.

The 1990 National Assessment of Educational Progress (NAEP) concluded that "large proportions — perhaps more than half of our elementary, middle, and high school students — are unable to demonstrate competency in challenging subject matter in English, mathematics, science, history, and geography." Further, even fewer appear to be able to use their minds well.

More than a decade after *A Nation At Risk* drew attention to America's educational mediocrity, the reading proficiency of nine- and 13-year-olds has declined even further.

Only three percent of American fourth, eighth, and twelfth graders can write above a "minimal" or "adequate" level, according to the 1992 Writing Report Card.

The test, which rated students' writing abilities on a scale of one to six, found that fewer than one in 30 American children earned a score high enough to indicate they could write effectively or persuasively. That's only three percent!

Only one out of four students even managed to write at a "developed" level, which earned a score of four. Even the best students who could write effective narrative and informative pieces had difficulty writing persuasively, the study found.

Other studies confirm the low-levels of academic achievement by America's public school students:

Elementary

■ Only one in five nine-year-olds can perform even basic mathematical operations. Does that mean 80 percent of America's fourth graders can't add, subtract, or multiply?

■ According to the 1990 NAEP, only one in six nine-year-olds reads well enough to "search for specific information, interrelate ideas, and make generalizations."

■ Only one in four nine-year-olds can apply basic scientific information.

Junior High

■ Among American 13-year-olds, only one in ten can "find, understand, and summarize complicated information."

■ Only one in eight eighth graders can understand basic terms and historical relationships.

■ Only one in eight 13-year-olds can understand and apply intermediate scientific knowledge and principles.

Large proportions of students are unable to demonstrate competency in challenging subject matter.

High School

■ The 1994 NAEP found that a third of American 17-year-olds say they are not required to do homework on a daily basis.

■ Only one high school junior out of 50 (2 percent) can write well enough to meet national goals.

■ Less than ten percent of 17-year-olds can do rigorous academic work in basic subjects.

■ A reading report card finds that 25 percent of high school seniors can barely read their diplomas.

THE GRADUATES

What about the students who have graduated from this failed experiment in education? How are they fairing as adults?

■ A standardized test given to 26,000 Americans 16 and older "concluded that 80 million Americans are deficient in the basic reading and mathematical skills needed to perform rudimentary tasks in today's society."[12]

■ A 1993 study by the U. S. Department of Education found that 90 million adults — 47 percent of the population of the United States — demonstrates low levels of literacy.

■ The level of literacy among adults has fallen by four percent since 1986.

■ A survey by the Gallup Organization found that one in seven adults can't find the United States on a blank map of the world.

None of these results should be surprising compared to the poor "education" — I hesitate to use the word — America's high school graduates received at the hands of our enlightened educators.

This decline in educational performance goes beyond the individual's lack of skills to affect the workplace. American businesses are now spending $30 billion on worker's training and lose an estimated $25 billion a year as a result of their worker's weak reading and writing skills.

A survey by the National Association of Manufacturers found that nearly a third of American businesses said the learning skills of their workers are so low that they are unable to organize work responsibilities.

How can a child attend school for 12 years — 180 days a year for six hours a day — and not be prepared to enter society and get a job?

In some cases jobs are going begging because high school graduates are unqualified for many entry-level positions. Charles J. Sykes, in his book, *Dumbing Down Our Kids,* presents these horrifying facts:[13]

■ In late 1992, executives at Pacific Telesis found that 60 percent of the high school graduates applying for jobs at the firm failed a company exam at the seventh-grade level.

■ In a recent year, the Bellsouth Corporation in Atlanta found that fewer than ten percent of their job applicants met minimal levels of ability for sales, service, and technical jobs.

■ MCI Communications in Boston reported that some of its jobs were going unfilled because the company could not find enough qualified applicants.

How can a child attend school for 12 years — 180 days a year for six hours a day — and not be prepared to enter society and get a job? That's the question many parents are asking.

IS MORE MONEY THE ANSWER?

Writing in the *National Observer*, Jerrold Foutlick states, "New York City spends twice as much on education as it did six years ago, and the percentage of children below minimum comprehension in reading has increased."[14]

Time and again the public schools — and countless government studies — have proved that money has little to do with teacher performance or student achievement.

Will spending more money solve the problem of America's failing public schools? Not according to economist Eric Hanushek, who in 1989 published the results of over 200 studies on comparing the relationship between "the resources spent on schools and the performance of students."[15] He came to two undeniable conclusions:

■ There is no systematic relationship between expenditures on schools and students' performance.

■ There is no systematic relationship between the major ingredients of instructional expenditures per student — chiefly teacher education and teacher experience, which informally drive teacher salaries and class size — and student performance.

Has anything changed since 1989? Nothing except higher teacher salaries and lower student performance.

The United States spends more money on education than any other industrialized country, and the appeal to spend more continues. Yet we get less for our money, it appears, than any other nation.

The Economist, March 29, 1997, noted that the results of international academic testing showed that "six of the top 15 places in both math and science went to East Europeans." You know, those recently liberated countries where most kids have never seen a computer much less used one!

We spend more on education than any other industrialized country, yet we seem to get less for our money than any other nation.

American children have three times as much money spent on their schooling as young South Koreans who, nevertheless, beat them hands down. In math, we scored behind South Korea, Hong Kong, Belgium, and the Czech Republic, to name a few. In fact, American students were twenty-eighth in math.

In science, we came in number 17 — well below Russia, Slovakia, Australia, Belgium, Hungary, Austria — in spite of the fact that we spend more money than *all* other nations combined!

What's wrong with this picture? Either American teachers aren't teaching or American students are dumber than ever.

Students can't be the problem, however, since in New York City, 85 percent of parochial school graduates go on to college — while in public school the rate is 20 percent. And everyone knows that Catholic school teachers are paid far less than their public school counterparts.

And who can explain why 40 percent of the school children in Chicago have parents — or a single parent — who scrape together tuition money to send their children to parochial schools? Could it be because these church-run schools are safer, demand respect from their students, use firm discipline measures, and have higher standards of academic achievement?

THE BIG BUSINESS OF EDUCATION

What I don't understand is why parents and taxpayers haven't risen up in revolt. Why do we keep propping up this bumbling giant when it is obviously out of control and headed in the wrong direction?

Could it be because the public schools have become so entwined with American life and its economy that the community itself now depends on the system's very existence?

John Gatto thinks so and calls the schools "an enormous, remotely controlled commercial enterprise." In other words, schools are big business. According to Gatto:[16]

■ "Schools are the single largest employer in the United States." Consider the number of janitors, secretaries, bus drivers, crossing guards, teachers, principals, administrators, band directors, etc. needed to operate a single community's school system.

■ "Schools are the largest mediator of contracts." Buildings and facilities must be built, maintained, and renovated.

■ "Schools have powerful political friends and advocates." The National Education Association constantly lobbies congressmen and senators, and the Department of Education maintains a budget the size of some European nations.

■ Schools have tremendous purchasing power of everything from books to toilet paper.

It's hard to buck a system when Aunt Mary works in the school cafeteria, sister Jane teaches third grade, and the former high school football star is superintendent of the district. Besides, your neighbor was just awarded the contract to pave the junior high parking lot!

No wonder public education — with its abysmal record of failure — still thrives like a cancerous tumor eating off the healthy cells around it. Could it be that the public refuses to extricate the malignancy for fear everything around it will die, too?

Could this be why — no matter what the failure rate — public schools continue to produce an inferior product? After all, what are the consequences? A few angry school board members? A little bad publicity? That, too, will pass with lame promises of reform and the expectation that the taxpaying public will soon forget. And we don't disappoint them.

ENOUGH IS ENOUGH!

University president John Silber thinks it's past time for Americans to do more than complain. He explains where we are now and what we need to do:

The crisis of our schools is the crisis of our democracy. It will reach the point of disaster unless parents, educators, politicians, and citizens unite to reverse the trend and provide our children with dedicated teachers and excellent schools. America does not lack concern, intelligence, resources, manpower, or tradition. But the nation has not shown that it has the resolve without which we will lose the vision of what has made us great.[17]

What will it take for us to muster up enough resolve to say, "Enough is enough!"

One of the most encouraging indicators of positive change is the number of parents who — like the early Puritans — are stepping up to the plate to assume responsibility for the education of their children. In spite of the obstacles, it is still possible for America's parents to steal the lead from government educators and hit a run that will make it all the way home.

CHAPTER EIGHT

The NEA: Humanism's Ally

A friend of mine, who is a teacher in Minnesota, attended a seminar sponsored by the Minnesota Education Association (MEA) on "Recognizing the Radical Right." Afterwards, he sent me his notes.

I was astonished at the unbridled hatred these "educators" hold toward beliefs that form the bedrock of our culture.

Keep in mind that by "educators" I am referring to the educational elite — the union officials of the National Education Association (NEA) and the bureaucrats at the Department of Education. I know there are many God-fearing, moral, family-oriented teachers who daily take courageous stands for their faith and principles in the classroom and, as a result, make a tremendous impact on the lives of students.

Their task, however, is made even more difficult when the very union to which they belong — and to which they pay expensive dues — publishes guidelines like *Unmasking Religious Right Extremism.*

How does the Minnesota Education Association — the state branch of the NEA — define the "Radical Right"? As "extremists" who "lobby for legislation, organize to take over mainstream political parties, and run for political office at the national, state, and local levels."[1]

Why are educators so worried? Because, as this position paper states, "the Religious Right extremists' campaign of recent years to gain control of political parties, our government, and our schools poses a serious threat to this nation."

WHO ARE THE EXTREMISTS?

"Who are the extremists?" the union educators asked in their seminar.

"For the most part, they are a subgroup of evangelical Protestants and fundamentalists," the educators wrote.

Who are they describing? Evangelicals — the millions of Americans who believe salvation lies in faith, not good works — and fundamentalists — those who believe in a literal interpretation of the Bible. Until a generation ago, such God-fearing people were considered the "backbone of society" and not "radical extremists." In fact, most teachers themselves would have been among our ranks — and probably many are today.

Until a generation ago, such God-fearing people were considered the "backbone of society" and not "radical extremists."

This next accusation made about right-wing "extremists" is accurate: "They reject much of the public school curriculum saying it is imbued with 'secular humanist' and 'New Age' religious teaching."

Does the Minnesota's teacher's union deny it? Of course not. In fact, most teachers and educators are well aware of the left-wing propaganda being forced on America's school children.

The seminar went on to describe "Religious Right extremists" as those who:

■ Oppose "all sex education for students other than counseling abstinence before marriage. This rigid stance denies students education about pregnancy and sexually transmitted diseases."

■ Advocate "the teaching of creationism in place of evolution."

■ Oppose "most curricula emphasizing self-esteem, critical thinking, and problem solving, saying these are too equivocal on moral issues."[2]

All of these statements are true, I'm proud to say.

At least the officials of Minnesota's teachers' union (MEA) know where we stand. We must be making an impact. Otherwise, why would they hold a day-long seminar to prevent further fall-out among their own ranks?

One statement from the seminar paper caught my attention: "Extremists insist . . . on teaching absolute right and wrong."

Now there's a dangerous point of view — teaching right and wrong! It's hard to know whether to laugh or cry.

The MEA agenda began to gel when the educators described the "radical right's" view of the "family":

> The concept of family generally means only those traditional families in which father is the head and all members are related by blood or marriage. All other kinds of family — friends who live together, single mothers, single fathers, or homosexual partners — are, according to the Right, not families at all. Rather, their very existence is antifamily.

Remember, they are describing you and me. We are now the ones labeled "antifamily," when the MEA's main objective is to destroy the "traditional" family and substitute an all-inclusive "village" in which education "parents" our children from cradle to college.

NO CHRISTMAS TO REMEMBER

Every year the California Teachers' Association provides a calendar for its teachers, listing "Important Dates to Remember." Here are a few of the events selected for celebration:

August
9 — Mohammed's birthday
26 — Women's Equality Day
September
19 — Hispanic Heritage Month
22 — International Day of Peace and American Indian Day
October
11 — National Coming Out Day (when homosexuals "come out of the closet")
23 — Diwali (Hindu Festival of Lights)
24 — United Nations Day
31 — Halloween
November — American Indian Heritage Month
December
1 — World AIDS Day
6-31 — Kwanza
10 — International Human Rights Day
29 — Anniversary of the Massacre of the Sioux at Wounded Knee
January
22 — Ramadan (Muslim holy day)

February — Black History Month
   20 — Shawwal (Muslim holy day)
March — Women's History Month
   8 — National Women's Day
   15 — Buddha's Nirvana Day
April
   28 — Dhu'l-Hijja (Muslim holy day)
   1-30 — Mahavira Birthday (Founder of
      Jainism)
May — Asian/Pacific Heritage Month
   5 — Japanese Children's Day
   7 — Buddha's birthday
   18 — Muharram (Muslim holy day)
June — Gay and Lesbian Pride Month
   2 — American Indian Citizenship Day
   27-28 — Stonewall Rebellion Anniversary

What is this last great event of the school year? The police raid on the Stonewall gay bar — well-known for illegal sexual behavior — on Christopher Street in New York. On this day, gays and lesbians came out of the closet determined never to go back. Also known as "Gay Pride" day, the date is celebrated in cities throughout the United States, often with the blessing of local city councils.

While California's school children are reminded to honor the homosexuals who resisted arrest at the Stonewall gay bar, other important historical and religious events are ignored.

There is no mention of European History Month — no day to celebrate Western Civilization, which gave the world the greatest country in the history of the earth. Although Buddha's birthday and Muslim and Hindu holy days are commemorated, Christmas — the birthday of Jesus — didn't even make the list!

Let's face it: America's schools have expelled Christianity. Educators make no secret of their hostility toward revealed religion. Although they make a claim of neutrality, it is no longer valid. Instead, the educational elite have crossed the line and substituted another religion — secular humanism — for the faith of our fathers.

How much longer will Americans support an educational bureaucracy that wages open warfare against God?

The educational elite have crossed the line and substituted another religion — secular humanism — for the faith of our fathers.

CHILDREN AS FODDER

"Atheists have taken over public education in the U. S.," warns Dr. Weldon Shoftstall, an Arizona educator. "Public schools are becoming more and more atheistic."

Why is that? Dr. Shoftstall explains that many educators believe "religion is exclusively a personal matter." They think that "separation of church and state includes separation of religion and education." Added to this misconception is the "acceptance of collectivism in the name of individualism, and an acceptance of humanism as theism."[3]

Al Janney, president of the American Association of Christian Schools, warns that "the gap between the Bible and the world is getting larger all the time." What are the consequences of this gap? Dr. Janney writes:

For many years, the public schools taught character education and reinforced the Protestant ethics that grew out of the Word of God. Now the public school is making a frontal attack on the Protestant ethics; therefore, we had better answer their charges. And they make their attack by using our children: the young are the fodder for their mills, and the young come from us. They use our children to form a secular-humanistic America.[4]

What makes Mr. Janney think that the public schools are using humanism to mold the minds of America's students? Because many educators have adopted the same tenets as *The Humanist Manifesto*, which considers religion to hold "doctrines and methods which have lost their significance and which are powerless to solve the problem of humans living in the 20th century."

At the same time, this Manifesto calls for "widespread recognition of the radical changes in religious beliefs throughout the modern world... and it is... obvious that any religion that can hope to be a synthesizing and dynamic force for today must be shaped for the needs of this age."[5]

Guess who wants to do the shaping.

**The lies of humanism are kept
alive 180 days every year in
every classroom across America.**

KEEPING HUMANISM ALIVE

Without public education, the myth of humanism would have been dead and buried long ago. Instead, its lies are kept alive 180 days every year in every classroom across America.

"Education is the most powerful ally of humanism," wrote Charles Francis Potter in his 1930 publication, *Humanism: A New Religion,* in which he proclaimed:

What can the theistic Sunday schools, meeting for an hour once a week, and teaching only a fraction of the children, do to stem the tide of a five-day program of humanistic teaching?[6]

Mr. Potter is not alone in his desire to use public education to brainwash America's children. In fact, the humanist philosophy has its greatest advocate in America's largest labor union.

How do we know? Because the National Education Association's (NEA) own resolutions state:

> The Association ... believes that legislation and regulations that mandate the teaching of religious doctrines, such as so-called "creation science," violate both student and teacher rights. The Association urges its affiliates to seek repeal of such mandates where they exist.[7]

Brock Chisholm, former director-general of the World Health Organization, writing in the journal, *Psychiatry*, calls for "a program of re-education or a new kind of education." Why? So the "science of living" can be "made available to all people." How? By teaching it "to all children in primary and secondary schools."

For what purpose? To "help our children to carry out their responsibilities as world citizens as we have not been able to do," Mr. Chisholm states.

The ultimate goal? "To achieve world government."

How will that be accomplished? By removing "from the minds of men their individualism, loyalty to family tradition, national patriotism, and religious dogmas."

Mr. Chisholm also believes that Americans "have swallowed all manner of poisonous certainties fed us by our priests."

What does he propose in its place? He unashamedly states the objectives for "charting changes in human behavior":

■ The "reinterpretation and eventual eradication of the concept of right and wrong which has been the basis of child training."

■ The "substitution of intelligent and rational thinking for faith in the certainties of the old people."[8]

Mr. Chisholm wants to eradicate the concept of right and wrong in our children's minds by "re-educating" them in the public schools and substituting faith in God for "rational thinking."

AIMING FOR THE CHILDREN

What would the American people do if they were told: Humanist educators plan to destroy the values parents are instilling in their children, "re-educate" them with godless philosophies — and ultimately gain control of the country?

Surely, there would be a national outcry! Surely, American parents would be up in arms and outraged!

Do the humanists try to hide their agenda? No. In fact, humanists have paraded their goals and their beliefs before us for years, and barely a whimper — much less an outcry — has yet to be heard.

As long ago as 1977, in the January/February issue of *The Humanist,* Sidney Hook (signer of the 1973 *Humanist Manifesto*) wrote:

> Human beings can be influenced to examine critically their religious beliefs only by . . . a critical attitude in all our educational institutions that will aim to make students less credulous to claims that transcend their reflective experience.[9]

What vehicle do the humanists plan to use to force this examination of religious beliefs? Our "educational institutions." The humanists' target? Your children.

In fact, Paul Blanchard, in an article in *The Humanist,* March/April 1976, makes it clear that the humanists' goal is to keep your children under their influence — and away from you as parents — as long as possible:

> I think the most important factor leading us to a secular society has been the educational factor. Our schools may not teach Johnny to read properly, but the fact that Johnny is in school until he is 16 tends to lead toward the elimination of religious superstition. The average child now acquires a high school education, and this militates against Adam and Eve and all other myths of alleged history.[10]

The goal of humanism is clear: Eliminate God and all religious beliefs and biblical teaching from the minds of students.

Humanists want to keep your children under their influence — and away from you — as long as possible.

What is humanism's replacement for God? Man.

"Man is at last becoming aware that he alone is responsible for the realization of the world of his dreams, that he has within himself the power for its achievement," the *Humanist Manifesto* explains.

What is man's purpose in life? ". . . the complete realization of human personality [is] to be the end of man's life and . . . its development and fulfillment in the here and now."[11]

Whatever happened to the Westminster Catechism, in which "the chief end of man is to love God and fully to enjoy Him forever"?

POLITICALLY HYPER-ACTIVE

"Welcome to the headquarters of the National Education Association," the brochure reads as visitors are invited to a self-guided walking tour of the NEA Center in Washington, D.C.

During my visit, I found the NEA's Commemorative Collage of interest. Designed by a local artist, the photos, news articles, and memorabilia chronicle the NEA's history and provide information on the goals and activities of the association.

One of the newspaper articles captured my attention: "Political Involvement is a Hallmark of the NEA From its Inception."

Why political involvement? I wondered.

As I read, the article explained the NEA's major political goal: To "place education at the center of the national agenda."

Author and educator Phoebe Courtney notes:

Today, less than four percent of NEA's vast annual budget is actually spent on instruction and professional development. All the rest is poured into maintaining and expanding the union's dominating control over the American educational debacle.[12]

Over the years, the NEA has had many successes, having achieved the "right of its members to organize and participate in politics."

The NEA also campaigned for an Equal Rights Amendment and helped fund UNESCO (United Nations Educational, Scientific, and Cultural Organization), which would "become the preeminent international sponsor of educational activities."

One of the NEA's greatest achievements came when President Jimmy Carter established the U. S.

Department of Education and made the Secretary of Education a member of the President's Cabinet.

Few Americans realized at the time the power and control the huge Department of Education would exhibit over our nation's public schools — to the point where local school boards merely carry out the edicts of Washington's education bureaucrats.

And guess who exerts tremendous influence on the Department of Education. That's right — the National Education Association.

Most significant is the NEA-PAC — a political action committee which "allows the NEA to influence the national legislative agenda, shape electoral platforms, and lend support to candidates with positions favorable to public education."

Funded by member contributions, NEA-PAC has become "one of the nation's largest and most influential" political action groups.

In his State of the Union Address, President Clinton declared to ringing applause, "Politics must end at the schoolhouse door."

That's not what Sam Lambert, executive secretary of the National Education Association, had in mind when he predicted in 1967:

> The NEA will become a political power second to no other special interest group. . . . NEA will organize this profession from top to bottom into logical operational units that can move swiftly

214 *Aim for the Children*

and effectively and with power unmatched by any other organized group in the nation.[13]

A survey by the National Center for Education Information shows that among public school teachers:

- 42 percent are Democrats.
- 30 percent are Republicans.
- 28 percent are Independents.

In the 1996 presidential campaign, the NEA spent $2.3 million. (The other union, the American Federation of Teachers spent $1.6 million.) Guess how much of that money went to Democratic candidates? Ninety-nine percent![14]

Looks like the schoolhouse door is wide open to anyone who supports the NEA's political agenda.

"RIGHTS FOR ALL"?

During my visit to the NEA national headquarters, I came across their Mission Statement and obtained more insight into their objectives for America:

To fulfill the promise of a democratic society, The National Education Association shall promote the cause of quality education and advance the profession of education; expand the rights and further the interests of educational employees; and advocate human, civil, and economic rights for all.[15]

The words "rights for all" took on new meaning when I noticed a large and impressive award from GLAAD — the Gay and Lesbian Alliance Against Defamation — which had been presented to the NEA. I'm sure it was well-deserved since the NEA not only supports gay rights but advocates — even mandates — the teaching of homosexuality as an appropriate lifestyle to America's children.

After I had studied the collage and arrived at the last room of the visitor's gallery, the thought occurred to me: I have repeatedly seen the words "democracy," "civil rights," "human rights," "equal rights," "gender equality," "political force" — but not one mention of "religious freedom" or God!

"And why should there be?" you ask. Because early American education was predicated on the existence and importance of God.

In the year the Constitution was written in Philadelphia (1787), Congress passed the Northwest Ordinance, Article 3, which reads:

Religion, morality, and knowledge, being necessary to good government and the happiness of mankind, schools and the means of education shall forever be encouraged.

Our Founding Fathers wanted to make sure that, as the nation reached westward, the people would open schools for the children, and that religion and morality would be combined with every other discipline to create a trained, knowledgeable civil nation.

The NEA, however, has other plans.

Many educators consider parents as their greatest threat to undermining the NEA's goal of molding children into a society of people they can control.

YOU ARE THE ENEMY!

The educational elitists ridicule the idea of the "traditional family" with a stay-at-home mom, a father who is the head of the household, and family members who are related by blood or marriage.

Why would the NEA want to trample on the biblical concept of family that has worked in America for 300 years — and around the world for millenniums?

By and large, the educationists would like to get parents out of the way. Why do you think the concept of kindergarten was born? Because educators believed that the sooner children were removed from parental influence, the better.

Many educators consider parents as their greatest threat to undermining the NEA's goal of molding children into a society of people they can control. When parents begin to question textbook content and teaching methods, the educators run to plug every hole in the dike.

"Public education is currently encountering criticism of unusual intensity and scope," wrote Hollis L. Caswell, dean of The Teachers College. "The disposition of laymen [i.e., parents] to invade the professional field of selection of instructional materials is a threat to sound curriculum development."

How should such criticism be handled? Mr. Caswell suggests that attacks on textbooks "must be met with calm, constructive, and courageous action."

In 1955, the *NEA Journal* published an article that stated:

A dramatic speech in 1950 by Harold Benjamin, then chairman of the Defense Commission, alerted the profession to a threatening new wave of deceitful and destructive criticism of public education. His address, "Report on the Enemy," sought to awaken the public and the teaching profession.[16]

How did the NEA plan to combat the public's criticism and prevent such organized attacks from damaging their credibility? "The NEA Defense Commission," the NEA article continued, "has collected information concerning the background, nature, and purpose of certain organizations engaged in spreading propaganda."

Get this straight: If you are an evangelical Christian, a devout Catholic, or a faithful, religious Jew — if you believe in free enterprise, if you love freedom, if you are committed to such ancient ideas as chastity, good manners, absolute honesty — you are the enemy!

TURNING CHILDREN AGAINST PARENTS

In her book, *Brave New Schools,* Berit Kjos writes about the strategies used by educators to turn children against their parents. "Multicultural and environmental education" is being used as a vehicle for change along with "strategies for sex and AIDS education."

For what purpose? To confuse a child's values and fuel "rebellion against traditional authorities."

As an example, Kjos relates this disturbing account of treachery:

When Kim Shaw signed a permission slip allowing her daughter to attend an AIDS-awareness seminar at Hale Middle School, she had no idea that her 12-year-old would be exposed to explicit descriptions of sex acts. If she had known that the seventh and eighth graders would learn practical ways to apply condoms in order to enjoy premarital sex without consequences, she would never have signed. Worst of all, the seventh and eighth graders were coached to hide their sexual activity from their parents and reject their home-taught values.

Shaw said, "I felt it went too far in giving graphic details. But what I was most upset about was how they taught them to cheat and lie to their parents. They told them how to hide their condoms and their wrappers after they were done with them. They said, 'You have to make sure your parents don't find them.'

"Two pamphlets were given to the students. One showed how to use condoms. The other was titled '100 Ways to Make Love Without Doing It.'"[17]

This is only one dramatic example.

In Pennsylvania, an organization called Commonwealth Education Organization (CEO) has become an education watch-dog for parents concerned about privacy issues.

CEO now has a file several inches thick of school "questionnaires" that were given to children. Personal questions were asked about students' family life: Do your parents argue? Do they smoke? Do they drink? How do they discipline you? What magazines do you have in your home? What did you have for dinner last night?

The children were then instructed not to tell their parents about the questionnaires. When parents called the school to complain, administrators offered no apologies and as much as said, "It's none of your business!"

Outraged parents are now trying to have Pennsylvania's legislators pass a bill mandating that "informed, parental consent" notifications be issued before any questionnaires or "psychological testing" can be administered to children.

WHO OWNS THE CHILDREN?

Newsweek recently published an article titled *Education in America,* in which Pat Henry, National PTA President, praised "Hillary Rodham Clinton's long history of involvement in children's issues."

Henry went on to emphasize the importance of parental involvement, but then said, "But we can't leave it to the parents. We can't leave it to schools. You and I must get involved."

Who has the ultimate authority over a child, the parents or the state? The trend in much of Outcome Based Education and Goals 2000 moves parents out of the way.

Who owns our children? Who has the right to educate them?

The State of Ohio thinks they do. Their legislators passed a law stating:

The natural rights of parents to custody and control of their children are subordinate to the power of the state to provide for the education of such infant children. Laws providing for the education of children are for the protection of the state itself.

Elmer Towns notes, "Compulsory attendance laws may become the Trojan horse that tips our nation into godlessness."

In other words, by using legal means to force your children to attend school — at any age the government prescribes — parents will be mandated to turn their toddlers over to the state.

WHEN YOU WALK BY THE WAY

God has given the responsibility of the child's education to parents: "Train up a child in the way he should go, and when he is old he will not depart from it" (Proverbs 22:6).

The Hebrew family was given the *Shema,* their greatest commandment: "Hear, O Israel: The Lord our God, the Lord is one! You shall love the Lord your God with all your heart, with all your soul, and with all your might" (Deut. 6:4,5).

This commandment was so important that God said:

These words which I command you today shall be in your heart; you shall teach them diligently to your children, and shall talk of them when you sit in your house, when you walk by the way, when you lie down, and when you rise up (Deut. 6:6,7).

God prescribes this commandment to be kept before the eyes of the children and written on the doorpost of their house, lest they forget the Lord who brought them out of the bondage of Egypt (Deut. 6:8-12).

Education is the responsibility of parents, as the New Testament commands: "Children, obey your parents in the Lord" (Eph. 6:1). Fathers are commanded, "Bring them [children] up in the training and admonition of the Lord" (Eph. 6:4).

"Whether the parent did the actual instruction, or saw that the child went to the temple where the rabbi could teach them, education was primarily a parental responsibility. To support the Levites, priests, and rabbis, parents paid their tithe to the temple.

"When a child did not obey, the parent was held responsible, as in the case of the priest Eli. He was judged because he did not rear his children properly (1 Sam. 2:12-17, 22-25; 4:17,18).

"When the nation of Israel was taken into captivity, God reminded them that the sins of the parents would be visited upon the children (Deut. 5:9)," notes Elmer Towns.[18]

Who is raising your children?

Two equally important questions to ask are: What kind of parents will your children make? Will they raise their children according to biblical principles or according to the tenets of humanism?

TYRANTS AS SCHOOLMASTERS?

Where are we now? Do parents have a chance to rescue their children before it's too late?

Elmer Towns sums up his thoughts:

First the church lost its place in the schools. Next, God was dispensed from the classroom; and during the last generation, the public schools have lost their character. Therefore, we ask, "Have the public schools 'had it'?"[19]

How long will American citizens continue to support public schools and universities that undermine the student's faith, ridicule their parents, and criticize their government and way of life?

What's the point of bringing children into the world, nurturing them, supporting them, loving them, and sacrificing to pay for their education if the educational institutions are going to separate them from the values and beliefs of their parents?

How long will we support public schools and universities that undermine the student's faith, ridicule their parents, and criticize their government and way of life?

David Harmer writes in *School Choice,* "It is becoming increasingly difficult to exaggerate the magnitude of the disaster in the government schools."[20]

Could it be that Alexis de Tocqueville was right when he foresaw the potential despotisms that lay in our future: "I do not expect their leaders to be tyrants, but rather schoolmasters."[21]

TIME TO BE RADICAL?

If evangelical Christians are going to be branded "radical" and "extremist," maybe we should start living up to that reputation.

Perhaps the time has come to *be* radical, to embrace some disciplines in our personal lives, to rebuild the Christian home, to teach our children that it is all right to be different.

Let's strive to replicate the perseverance of the handful of first-century believers. Having been scattered by persecution, they refused to succumb to the culture around them and, instead, built a subculture within it.

One observer wrote that these radical Christians had "out-thought, out-lived, and out-died" their contemporaries, and by the end of the third century had overturned paganism and, at least in name, built a Christian world.

On a small plaque in front of the historic Park Street Church in Boston are these words:

On July 4, 1829, William Lloyd Garrison delivered his first anti-slavery speech here and so launched his emancipation campaign with the words, "Since the cause of emancipation must progress heavily, and must meet with much unhallowed opposition — why delay the work?"

I propose a similar question to us today: Since the freeing of our children from a godless educational system will surely meet with great opposition — what are we waiting for? Why delay the work?

Why wait until our children are so enslaved that we can no longer wrench them from their oppressors' clutches?

CHAPTER NINE

Outcomes or Lost Opportunities?

When I first heard the term "outcome-based education," I asked: "What is OBE? Is this something I should be for or against?"

I didn't want to rush to judgment like the mother who yells down the hall, "See what the kids are doing and tell them to quit."

In that case, you assess the nature of the children's conduct before demanding they stop doing it. Maybe all they're doing is breathing.

There is no merit in opposing ideas, programs, and initiatives for the sake of being against something. That is why some questions must be asked if we are to arrive at a responsible position relative to a concept that will affect America's children one way or the other:

- What is outcome-based education?
- Whose idea was it?
- What is the desired outcome?
- Who decides, and by what criteria, if the desired outcome has been achieved?

Dr. William Spady, director of the International Center on Outcome-Based Restructuring, coined the phrase "Outcome-Based Education." He defines OBE as a means of "focusing and organizing all of the schools' programs and instructional efforts around clearly defined outcomes we want all students to demonstrate when they leave school."[1]

What are the desired outcomes of OBE?
The answers may surprise you.

No problem. Education *is* outcome. Without measurable results, education dollars and teachers' efforts would be wasted. The important question is: What is the desired outcome?

Phyllis Schlafly of the Eagle's Forum, who has studied Outcome-Based Education and its effects on students, says OBE "calls for a complete change in the way children are taught, graded, and graduated, kindergarten though twelfth grade."[2]

EDUCATORS OR PSYCHOLOGISTS?

Twenty years ago, OBE was implemented in the Chicago city schools under the name Mastery Learning. The result can only be described as an unmitigated disaster.

- Almost half of the 39,000 students who began the program failed to graduate from high school.
- 18,000 inner city students dropped out of school.
- Two-thirds of those who graduated were unable to read at or above the national twelfth-grade level.[3]

And what did the teachers think of the program? Forty-four percent of them sent their children to private schools.

"The Chicago experiment in the 1970s with Professor Benjamin Bloom's Mastery Learning (ML)," Phyllis Schlafly notes, "was a colossal failure and was abandoned in disgrace in 1982. The test scores proved to be appallingly low, and the literacy rate became a national scandal."[4]

**OBE doesn't deal with academics.
It focues instead on feelings,
beliefs, and attitudes.**

Why weren't Chicago students learning? Because Mastery Learning and its successor OBE don't deal with academics; they focus instead on feelings, beliefs, and attitudes. Bloom himself has stated that "the purpose of education is to change the thoughts, feelings, and actions of students."

Sounds more like religion and psychology than reading and writing.

A friend of mine was serving on a local education committee in Oregon when the Oregon Educational Reform Act was introduced and passed. Troubled by the content of the legislation, he quizzed the representative who was pushing it through the state legislature.

My friend asked her, "Was this program developed by educators or by psychologists?"

The state representative refused several opportunities to answer. When pressed, she exploded, using the most offensive language to describe my friend and others who shared his point of view.

When she finished her tirade, my friend replied, "You just answered my question."

MEDIOCRITY NOT EXCELLENCE

While paging through a recent catalog from the National Education Association, I noticed that most of the literature emphasized "group building, nurturing self-esteem, social skills, communicating effectively, cooperation and play, and decision making."

For example, *Cooperative Learning in the Elementary Classroom* is a practical step-by-step approach to cooperative learning. What do teachers gain from this technique? "You'll learn how to build social skills and teach conflict management. . . . In addition, you'll discover how cooperative learning links to whole language, critical thinking, portfolio assessment, and classroom diversity."

Sounds impressive and very complicated. Such terminology, however, serves as a smoke screen to throw parents and legislators off track. The idea is to keep the methodology so ambiguous and illusive that opponents will give up trying to figure it out. Unfortunately, many states have capitulated — some were buffaloed by high-stepping educators; others caved in to pressure from the NEA and the federally funded Department of Education.

So what do OBE terms like "higher order thinking skills" or "critical thinking" really mean? They are actually the process of getting students to question moral values. What about the phrase "new basics"? Don't be fooled. That does not mean reading, writing, and arithmetic but OBE's predetermined attitudes and outcomes.

Students demonstrate "success" in the dumbed-down outcomes that the slowest learners in the class can attain.

This is exactly what John Dewey had in mind. Rather than teach children to read well and excel in the pursuit of the academics, the emphasis was on socializing them.

"Success" for all children means students have demonstrated "success" in the dumbed-down outcomes that the slowest learners in the class can attain. OBE means "success" in mediocrity rather than excellence.

That's why comedienne Tracey Ullman returned to England to educate her daughter. She explains:

> In California . . . everything is so-o-o touchy-feely. They are into this Outcome-Based Education, where it doesn't matter if she knew how to spell her name as long as she knew who she was. And it didn't matter if she knew that two plus two was four as long as she had enough self-confidence to ask how to get "to the conclusion of the problem." What a crock! She was going to end up as dumb as a mudflap.[5]

According to Phyllis Schlafly, OBE fails to teach first graders how to read. Why? Because OBE is committed to the "whole language" approach, which means the "word-guessing method" rather that the phonics method. As a result, children memorize only a few words that are repeated over and over, meaning they will be severely handicapped when it comes to reading more difficult material.

What about spelling? "Teachers are cautioned not to correct spelling and syntax errors because that could be damaging to the student's self-esteem and creativity," notes Schlafly. "OBE graduates will never be able to aspire to enjoy the great literature in the English language."[6]

EDUCATING OR TRAINING?

What is the difference between "educating" and "training"? In education, the teacher imparts knowledge and teaches facts along with content. In training, the "facilitator" relies on the rewards/punishments of Skinner and Pavlov. You know, the way you housebreak your new puppy or train the parakeet to sing.

In other words, teachers bypass the brain and rely on feelings and don't stop the "technique" until the child achieves "mastery" and automatically responds without thinking. The result: Students say, do, and believe what their "masters" want them to believe.

Students cannot progress until they submit — or are brainwashed — and give the expected response.

Professor Benjamin Bloom introduced Mastery Learning, which uses behavior-modification techniques like "stimulus, response, assessment, and remediation." Why? "To change the students' beliefs, attitudes, values, and behavior." How is this done?

"The student must 'master' each sequential step toward the required 'outcome' (and demonstrate this mastery by modifying behavior) before advancing to the next stage."[7]

In other words, students cannot progress until they submit — or are brainwashed — and give the expected response.

What is the purpose of OBE's Skinnerian conditioning or behavior modification? "To create 21st century, politically correct, compliant workers," suggests education researcher Pam Hoffecker.

What's wrong with Outcome-Based Education? Consider these consequences of OBE:[8]

■ De-emphasizes academics and focuses on changing behavior, attitudes, and feelings.

■ Holds top achievers back from further learning by making them teach the slower students.

■ Performs psychological tests on your children.

■ Keeps your children from graduating if they disagree with the values taught in the school.

■ Forces 15- and 16-year-old students to make career decisions.

■ Is astronomically expensive.

Dana Mack, writing in *The Assault on Parenthood: How Our Culture Undermines the Family*, explains OBE's impact on students:

Parents believe OBE . . . epitomizes the worst of the educational trend toward leveling academic accomplishment as well as its insidious tendencies toward psycho-social engineering. But children as well resent what they consider a dumbing down of the curriculum to allow the least capable child to achieve the outcome. Bright children who quickly master OBE academic outcomes typically spend their class time "peer-tutoring" their classmates rather than moving on. This can lead to long-term frustrations for the child who wants to and can learn.[9]

What about the 44 percent of Chicago teachers who placed their own children in private schools? Were these taxpayer funded teachers so troubled by what they were doing that they didn't want their own children involved in it?

How would you feel if a restaurant owner wouldn't eat his own food, or if the CEO of an airline wouldn't fly in one of his airplanes? It would give you pause, wouldn't it?

EDUCATIONAL DISARMAMENT

After the "unmitigated disaster" of the Chicago experiment, the national Commission of Excellence in Education was created on August 26, 1981, to look into the problem of declining test scores and increasing illiteracy. By April 1983, the Commission published a report called *A Nation At Risk: The Imperative for Education Reform.* It reads:

Our nation is at risk. We report to the American people that, while we can take justifiable pride in what our schools and colleges have historically accomplished and contributed to the United States and the well-being of its people, the educational foundations of our society are presently being eroded by a rising tide of mediocrity that threatens our very future as a nation and as a people.

What was unimaginable a generation ago has begun to occur — others are matching and surpassing our educational attainments. If an unfriendly foreign power had attempted to impose on America the mediocre educational performance that exists today, we might well have viewed it as an act of war. As it stands, we have allowed this to happen to ourselves. We have even squandered the gains in student achievement made in the wake of the Sputnik challenge. Moreover, we have dismantled essential support systems which helped make those gains possible. We have, in effect, been committing an act of unthinking, unilateral educational disarmament.[10]

After this absolutely scathing report on OBE, educators decided to abandon the obviously flawed and unproductive program, right? Not a chance. Instead, Dr. Spady, one of OBE's originators, reinforces the direct link of outcome-based education to

Blooms' relativistic, behavior-changing Mastery Learning. In his own words, Dr. Spady tells how he proposed a way to side-step the negative publicity of the Chicago project:

> In January 1980, we convened a meeting of 42 people to form the Network for Outcome-Based Schools. Most of the people who were there had a strong background in Mastery Learning, since it was what OBE was called at the time. But I pleaded with the group not to use the name "mastery learning" in the network's new name because the word "mastery" had already been destroyed through poor implementation.[11]

Instead of blaming OBE for the Chicago disaster, Spady faulted the teachers and school administrators. In an effort to retain the program, he suggested simply changing the name.

"I talk about two kinds of profound changes that need to happen if the system is going to be seriously outcome-based," Dr. Spady said later. "One is, you have to stop being time-based. The second is to stop being curriculum-based."[12]

What does Dr. Spady mean? That OBE planners hope to eliminate the school calendar mentality, increase the length of classes, and extend the school year. In other words, no matter how long it takes, "students must demonstrate with portfolios, productions, and assessments that they have reached state outcomes." In fact, achieving outcomes "may include extended days, weeks, or years," according to a bill passed by Kentucky legislators.[13]

If an unfriendly foreign power had attempted to impose on America the mediocre educational performance that exists today, we might well have viewed it as an act of war.

OBE promoters also plan to remove other tried-and-true educational standards like graded classrooms. By blending pre-kindergarten through third grade, and later grades four through 12, students will learn in multi-aged groupings according to individual progress and remediation.

TOTALLY TRANSFORMING SOCIETY

Shirley McCune, senior director of the Mid-Continent Regional Educational Laboratory — one of several research and curriculum development nerve centers funded by your tax dollars through the Department of Education — explains her goal to totally "transform society." Speaking at the national Governors' Conference on Education, she explains the goals of the educational elite:

What we're into is the total restructuring of society. What is happening in America today . . .

is not simply a chance situation in the usual winds of change. It amounts to a total transformation of society. You can't get away from it. You can't go into the rural areas, you can't go into the churches, you can't go into the government or into the businesses and hide.[14]

There it is in their own words: They plan to restructure society — totally transform America — and they are counting on our quiet acceptance of their schemes.

Ms. McCune's ideology is not an isolated opinion by any means. In fact, the goal of transforming society into an "equalized" utopia is reflected and espoused in the writings of many education and government policy makers today.

The National Training Laboratories (NTL), once an arm of the NEA and now an independent organization working toward the same purpose, suggests ways to influence human behavior. In the NTL publication, *Issues in Human Relations Training,* the editors write how human relations or "sensitivity training" fits into "a context of institutional influence procedures." That's a big name for ways to indoctrinate anyone who disagrees with them.

What outcomes do they expect from these "procedures"? One is "coercive persuasion in the form of thought information about 'change-agent skills' and 'unfreezing, changing and refreezing attitudes.'"[15] In other words, they hope to coerce the American public into changing their attitudes about what education is and how it should be accomplished.

David Jenkins' essay in the same NTL journal explains that the "laboratories" conducted by the NTL have recently moved from an emphasis on skill training to "sensitivity training." Jenkins declares that "the trainer has no alternative but to manipulate; his job is to pan and produce behavior in order to create changes in other people."[16]

There it is again. Manipulating people to produce a change in their behavior.

Regarding children, the journal states that while kids "appear to behave appropriately . . . this appearance is deceptive. . . . We are pseudo-healthy persons who can benefit from sensitivity training."

Are your children being manipulated through classroom "sensitivity training"? Probably, if they attend public school. And, unless you ask a lot of questions, you may never know what is really going on in America's little "laboratories."

THE GREAT DECEPTION

To camouflage their agenda, America's "agents of change" must deceive the public as Massell Smith advises in an article from a 1997 issue of the NTL publication, *Social Change:* "Couch the language of change in the language of the status quo. They are almost broad enough to encompass innovation."[17]

Educators purposely try to deceive by using "double-entendre expressions that parents assume mean one thing but really mean something different in the OBE context," notes Phyllis Schlafly.

Why the need for deceptive tactics? To keep parents from interfering with programs designed by the education elite.

John Goodlad, a professor at the University of Washington and president of the Institute for Educational Renewal, writes of the potential conflict between the new "values" educators are teaching children and those of the parents. In the preface to James Becker's book, *Schooling for a Global Age,* Goodlad writes why parents must be reeducated:

Parents and the general public must be reached. . . . Otherwise, children and youth enrolled in globally oriented programs may find themselves in conflict with values assumed in the home. And then the educational institution . . . comes under scrutiny.[18]

Why do educators fear scrutiny? Could it be because most Americans would be alarmed to discover the diabolical plans educators have for our children and youth?

In a report published by Goodlad, he cites the need to "resocialize" America's young people: "Most youth still hold the same values as their parents, and if we don't resocialize, our system will decay."[19]

What's wrong with the values of morality, integrity, faith in God, and hard work held by most American parents? Why the push to redefine what is right and wrong? Why the rush to escort God and faith out the back door?

Washington state Governor Gary Locke gives us a clue with this comment, "Education is the great equalizer that makes hope and opportunity possible."[20]

Think about that. When did parents abandon their commitment to educate and encourage each child to reach his fullest potential? Are parents supposed to stop challenging kids to be the unique persons God created them to be? Are we now to look toward education as a way to "equalize" everybody?

"AFTER THE SOCIALIST REVOLUTION"

Michael Lerner, a trusted associate of President and Mrs. Clinton, led the Seattle Liberation Front in the early 1970s — an ultra-left organization described by the Washington State attorney general as "totally indistinguishable from fascism and Nazism."

Lerner supports the idea of equalizing wealth as a way to eliminate America's social ills: "A rough equality in general wealth and income is a necessary condition for equality of political power. . . . Most of the crimes that we know today would simply disappear under a socialist society."[21]

How will such socialistic ideas be inculcated into American thinking? You guessed it! Through education. But not the kind of education you and I had.

Lerner suggests that students *not* be taught "isolated subjects" — like history, literature, science — or learn "isolated facts" — like how, when, why, and by whom our nation was founded. Instead, an "integrated viewpoint" will be encouraged that focuses on "actualizing talents and creativity."

The goal will be for students to "learn how to work and act together." The main emphasis of education "will be on learning how to play, how to create, how to be an individual, and how to live and work collectively."

Why are we teaching American kids to live and work collectively?

Collectively? Isn't that a term from an old Soviet textbook? Or maybe it's still a popular concept in China. But why are we teaching American kids to live and work collectively? What is going on?

Once again, President Clinton's friend, Michael Lerner, defines what they hope as the final purpose of education:

> After the socialist revolution, education will be a much broader role. Every community will begin to develop facilities for extensive educational opportunities in all areas of human intellectual life.[22]

After the "socialist revolution"! Surely, no one takes Mr. Lerner seriously. Or do they?

In 1988, then-governor Bill Clinton wrote Mr. Lerner, saying, "You have helped me clarify my own thinking."[23]

THE SEAMLESS WEB

The day after the 1992 presidential election, those of the socialist persuasion were beating their chests and already planning for the future. One such enthusiast, Marc Tucker, president of the National Center on Education and the Economy, wrote an 18-page letter to Hillary Rodham Clinton, which began:

> I still cannot believe you won. But utter delight that you did pervades all the circles in which I move. I met last Wednesday in David Rockefeller's office with him, John Sculley, Dave Barram, and David Heselkorn. It was a great celebration. Both John and David R. were more expansive than I have ever seen them — literally radiating happiness. My own view and theirs is that this country has seized its last chance. I am fond of quoting Winston Churchill to the effect that "America always does the right thing — after it has exhausted all the alternatives." This election, more than anything else in my experience, proves his point.[24]

In his letter to Mrs. Clinton, Mr. Tucker outlines how they plan to "create a seamless web of opportunities to develop one's skills that literally extends from cradle to grave."

How do they hope to achieve this uniform education system?

■ By controlling "curriculum, pedagogy, examinations, and teacher standards."

■ By requiring "institutions receiving grants and loan funds under this system . . . to provide information . . . that includes characteristics and career outcomes for those students."

■ By creating a "national Board for Professional and Technical Standards." According to Tucker, this board will be "private, not-for-profit, chartered by Congress. . . . Neither Congress nor the executive branch can dictate the standards set by the Board."[25]

In effect, this board will be accountable to no elected officials — not even the President.

How do Mr. Tucker and his cronies hope to achieve the "restructuring" of society? By creating a system of education based on "outcomes." This system would reward "students who meet the national standards with further education and good jobs."

What happens to those students who don't meet educators' ideological standards? Are they refused entrance into college and trade schools? Will they be unable to get a good job if they don't fit into the socialist mold?

TRACKING STUDENTS FOR LIFE

Every child educated under OBE is tracked through an "electronic portfolio," which takes the place of traditional assessments and test results. These "portfolios" indicate whether or not the student has "mastered" certain attitudes and behaviors that the school deems acceptable. In this one computer file, prospective employers can access all the students' academic, psychological, and medical records.

How will this be accomplished? Through OBE data banks and electronic information systems. Keep in mind that OBE focuses on learning outcomes (goals) that are basically the same in each state. Ohio's data banks already contain 93 categories on each student.

The danger with this electronic system is that over 50 percent of the learning outcomes students are expected to master are not academic but behavioral. Why? Because one of OBE's goals is to challenge "fixed beliefs" — including religious faith and traditional family values.

In other words, if your child is an independent thinker who reads his Bible and believes homosexuality and sex before marriage are immoral, he may receive an unsatisfactory rating for not conforming to OBE's government-mandated outcomes.

Will a child who has not demonstrated the OBE values and politically-correct attitudes be able to get a job? Not if state law forbids employers from hiring anyone who does not have "a certificate showing mastery of the government-mandated outcomes," Phyllis Schlafly notes. These "certificates" have already replaced high school diplomas in states such as Massachusetts, Oregon, and Washington.

**If students don't meet these outcomes,
will they be barred from college,
trade schools, and good jobs?**

According to the U. S. Department of Labor, "WORLDLINK will be an electronic information system linking local schools and employers."[26]

Don't miss the connection here. The U. S. government will maintain control over personal student information that will be passed from the schools to national and international businesses. Keep in mind this is the same government who mishandled the FBI files of hundreds of private American citizens for their own political purposes.

"Most Chinese live all their lives with files looming over them," notes the *New York Times*. The file is begun in school and "it shadows the person throughout life."[27]

Great! Now we're on par with China.

WHO NEEDS TO READ AND WRITE?

One of the touchstones of OBE and Goals 2000 is that all children will learn. But *what* will they learn?

Everything the social planners expect and want them to learn so they will fit into their socialist schemes. But don't expect Johnny to learn how to read or Susie to spell or Billy to add or subtract.

Why not? Because, as Harvard professor Anthony Oettinger explains, the elitist agenda is clear:

> The present "traditional" concept of literacy has to do with the ability to read and write. . . . But do we really want to teach people to do a lot of sums or write . . . when they have a five-dollar hand-held calculator or a word processor? . . . Do we really have to have everybody literate — writing and reading in the traditional sense?[28]

Hard to believe that a Harvard professor would suggest that reading and writing are mere relics of the past! Does Oettinger's statement mean that some Americans will be taught to read and others will be kept illiterate?

I am reminded of George Orwell's satire on the totalitarian state, *Animal Farm,* in which the animals overthrow the humans and take control of running the farm. The pigs, who were the smartest creatures, taught themselves to read and write using an old spelling book. With this new ability, they gained control over the other animals by making up regulations the illiterates couldn't read. As a result, the pigs changed the rules to suit their own selfish needs, and the other animals had no recourse but to obey them!

Thomas B. Sticht, president and senior scientist of Applied Behavioral and Cognitive Sciences, Inc., San Diego, California, is also a member of the U. S. Secretary of Labor's Commission on Achieving Necessary Skills (SCANS). Mr. Sticht writes that a labor force that can be easily managed is more important than having workers who can read:

> Many companies have moved operations to places with cheap, relatively poorly educated labor. What may be crucial, they say, is the dependability of a labor force and how well it can be managed and trained — not its general educational level, although a small cadre of highly educated, creative people is essential to innovation and growth. Ending discrimination and changing values are probably more important than reading and moving low-income families into the middle class.[29]

Are you beginning to get the picture? A small group of "highly educated, creative people" see themselves controlling a larger group of "poorly educated" workers. Do you see where America is headed?

CHAPTER TEN

The Road to Nowhere

Johnny can't read and Susie can't spell — and somebody planned it that way.

You may find that as hard to believe as I did until the facts revealed the truth: War has been declared against literacy.

My research was disconcerting. I could not figure out why students were failing academically in spite of educators' pleas for more funding. If the schools' methods are counterproductive, wouldn't spending more money simply provide for more miseducation?

I was puzzled why so many American kids could not read in a country that spends more on education than any other industrialized nation. How do you account for 24 million functional illiterates in the United States, most of whom have gone through 12 years of public education?

According to the *Washington Post,* if the reading portion of the 1996-1997 Stanford Achievement Test had been used to determine who passed and who failed, 33 percent of Washington D.C.'s third graders and 29 percent of eighth graders would be repeating their grade in September. Math scores were equally dismal: 33 percent of third graders and 75 percent of eighth graders scored below the norm.[1]

War has been declared against literacy.

Such scandalous results threaten our future as a nation. Our form of government and our very existence depend on an informed citizenry who can think, reason, and make rational judgments. How will the coming generations of Americans function in a democratic society if they are unable to read the newspaper and make change at the grocery story?

HOW HARD CAN IT BE?

In colonial America, parents taught their children to read at an early age. Such a feat was no mystery. To many pioneers giving their offspring the gift of reading was as important as teaching them to fish or hunt for food. It was a natural part of family life.

Why now, today, with the most expensive schools in history, fully unionized, with presidential and congressional support, are we passing children from grade to grade, failing to teach them to read?

How hard can it be? You start with the alphabet, then sound out the vowels and consonants, and arrange the letters together in words. During the first 200 years of our history, our forefathers taught their children to read without the aid of computer programs or high-tech reading laboratories.

Jonathan Edwards, the 18th century theologian and philosopher who spearheaded the Great Awakening, exemplifies the kind of education that made this country great.

> Jonathan's early education was supplied by his father, a gifted and exacting mentor whose thorough approach was largely responsible for his son's fastidious mind. The young man studied Greek at age five, learned Latin at age seven, and Hebrew by age 11, ultimately achieving mastery of all three languages. He was admitted to Yale at 13, and he graduated at the head of his class in 1720.[2]

Let's face it, few modern American kids are likely to be studying Greek at five or Latin at seven. But why after years of public schooling are many of them unable to read English well enough to function in modern society? These same kids — no less intelligent than youngsters who lived in the 1700s — can master complicated Nintendo games, recount the dialogue and story lines of dozens of movies, and memorize extended rap-song lyrics.

If the problem is not our students' ability to learn, then who is to blame?

Columnist Walter Williams provides the answer when he writes:

> Teachers and administrators are totally responsible for promoting kids who haven't mastered grade material and granting diplomas that attest a kid has achieved a twelfth-grade level of education when in fact he may not have achieved even an eighth-grade level. That is no less than open, pernicious fraud.[3]

Maybe educators have simply made a mistake and chosen the wrong teaching techniques. Surely, the Department of Education has made a concerted effort to ferret out the culprits, clean house, and get to the bottom of the literacy barrel.

I wish that were the case. Instead, our own taxpayer-funded government agencies continue to allow children to wander aimlessly through elementary and secondary school without the ability to read the map that directs them out of the maze.

THE EMPTY "EDUCATIONAL PIT"

As I dug deeper into the empty "educational pit," the same stone kept turning up. To my amazement,

the facts showed that America's illiteracy sinkhole
was planned — fostered by social planners who don't
trust the people, and who are determined to change
the character of this nation by "dumbing down" its
citizens.

**Johnny can't read and Susie can't spell
— and somebody planned it that way.**

The history of this assault on our national integrity
is not pleasant, but we must understand it if we are
to recover lost ground. Public education in America
goes well beyond the impartation of knowledge. In
fact, it discounts it; then takes a sinister turn in an
effort to modify children's behavior.

Like the behavioral scientist running rats through
a maze, America's social planners hope to keep
children locked in meaningless activity with only one
goal in mind: To turn them into obedient little
creatures who will fall in line and march to the
music. Keeping parents in the dark enables them to
achieve their diabolical ends more quickly and
without interference.

To understand how we ended up on the educational road to nowhere, we must go back and revisit
John Dewey, the "father of American education."

How did he view literacy? He makes no bones
about it: Reading was an obstacle to socialism.

These samplings from Dewey's writings clearly point out where he wanted to take American society:

> Too much emphasis cannot be laid upon the fact that undo premium is put upon the ability to learn to read at a certain chronological age. . . .
>
> It is one of the great mistakes in education to make reading and writing constitute the bulk of the school work the first two years.[4]

What did Dewey propose in place of teaching young children to read? Socialization.

> The true way is to teach them incidentally as the outgrowth of the social activities at this time. Thus, language is not primarily the expression of thought, but the means of social communication.[5]

Dewey thought that language ability resulted from "social activity" and was "an end in itself." He admitted, however, that the child will probably not "learn as much" or "as readily in a given period" as he would by "the usual method."

Although the notion has been disproved, Dewey thought the child would make "more rapid progress later when true language interest develops." Had that been true, by the time students graduate from high school they will have developed an "interest" and taught themselves to read. Funny how that has never happened.

"NO SOCIAL GAIN"

John Dewey, who had an agenda far removed from the best interests of our nation's young people, did not hide the fact that he despised "the private consciousness that seeks knowledge in order to exercise its own individual judgment and authority." The key words here are "knowledge" and "individual" — the stumbling blocks to socialism.

In *Democracy in Education,* published in 1916, John Dewey elaborates on this point:

> When knowledge is regarded as originating and developing within an individual, the ties which bind the mental life of one to that of his fellows are ignored and denied. When the social quality of individualized mental operations is denied, it becomes a problem to find connections which will unite an individual with his fellows.[6]

To promote his plan for social order, Dewey first had to dismantle the existing educational process and then convert educators to his way of thinking.

In *School and Society,* published in 1899, Dewey criticized the home-church-community type schooling that had so successfully educated Americans since the Pilgrims landed at Plymouth Rock:

The tragic weakness of the present school is that it endeavors to prepare future members of the social order in the medium in which the conditions of the social spirit are eminently wanting.[7]

Dewey considered "the mere absorbing of facts and truths" to be selfish on the part of the learner because there was no "social motive" or "social gain" involved in "the acquirement of mere learning."

In other words, learning for learning's sake is a useless activity if it does not benefit society as a whole.

A little later Dewey explained that the relegation of subject matter like science, art, and history "to a secondary position" — along with a "change in the moral school atmosphere" — "are not mere accidents, they are necessities of the larger social evolution." Once these changes in education were accomplished, all that remained was "to put the ideas and ideals involved to complete, uncompromising possession of our school system."

This is treason. To deliberately deny school children the opportunity to learn to read and to acquire knowledge reveals Dewey's contempt for the individual.

ILLITERACY AT ITS BEST

Dewey was not alone in his deception. Professor Nila Banton Smith, then professor of education at

New York University, also considered the method of teaching reading unimportant.

"We are on the brink of a new epoch in reading instruction," Smith wrote. "In the future reading instruction must concern itself with much more than pedagogy. It must mesh more directly with the gears of vital social problems and needs."[8]

This must be "the future" because illiteracy is definitely having an impact on American society.

Can you imagine teachers extolling the virtues of illiteracy?

It's hard to believe, but some consider illiteracy a bonus. G. Stanley Hall — a young American teacher and product of an orthodox New England family who totally succumbed to German influence — extolled the merits of illiteracy, including escape from "eye strain and mental excitement" and "certain temptations, such as vacuous and vicious reading." Those who can't read, Hall noted, were "more active and less sedentary."

Very many men have lived and died, and been great, even leaders of their age, without any acquaintance with letters. The knowledge which illiterates acquire is probably on the whole more personal, direct, environmental, and probably a much larger proportion of it, practical.[9]

It is possible for those who can't read "to lead a useful, happy, virtuous life" and "to be really well-educated in many other ways," as Mr. Hall suggests. Some who were unable to read have succeeded in life, but who would deny the enlargement of those successes through the pursuit of reading and the study of great literature?

"LOOK, JANE." "SEE, DICK."

The *Dick and Jane* series of reading primers contributed to "the new epoch in reading instruction" and gave us such brilliant, literary gems as:

Dick.
Look, Jane.
Look, Look.
See, Dick.
See, see.
Oh, see.
See, Dick. Oh, see, Dick.
Oh, oh, oh.
Funny, funny Dick.

This repetitive "look-say" word approach to teaching reading replaced the tried and trusted method of phonics. Instead of learning the alphabet and sounding out words, children were taught to look at a word with a picture and memorize it.

Earlier, we mentioned the *New England Primer,* which for 150 years was a primary text for America's children. This book taught the alphabet with a Bible verse after each letter and contained much of the Catechism. It inspired children to read and instructed them in essential principles for godly living.

The confusion between the "look-say" method of teaching and the method of phonics — which had been used for hundreds of years — produced serious reading problems in America's children and resulted in remedial courses in schools.

**The abandonment of phonics . . .
was a "time bomb" waiting to
explode in the nation's schools.**

In 1955, Rudolph Flesch wrote an important book titled, *Why Johnny Can't Read,* in which he answered the question many parents were asking about the elimination of phonics from reading programs.

Flesch warned in his best-selling book that the abandonment of phonics and other traditional approaches to reading was a "time bomb" waiting to explode in the nation's schools. Educators, however, ignored the alarms and the National Education Association thoroughly discredited Flesch. After all, the

NEA had to keep their teachers in line. The last thing they needed were educators jumping off the sinking ship.

The November 1955 issue of the *NEA Journal* criticized Flesch's book, dismissing it as "mostly opinion," with "quotations out of context," "limited personal observations," and "the occasional vicious rhetoric." Either Flesch is "deliberately attempting to mislead and deceive or Flesch can't read."[10] Rather than debate the issue or refute the message, the NEA simply ridiculed the messenger.

Later, Flesch wrote, "Twenty-five years ago, I studied American methods of teaching reading and warned against educational catastrophe. Now it has happened."

Instead of identifying the real problem — which was the method of teaching reading — the kids took the rap and an epidemic of "dyslexia" suddenly swept through America's classrooms.

In 1994, a magazine article noted:

Millions of children in the United States suffer from dyslexia, which is the medical term for reading difficulties. It is responsible for about 70 percent of the school failures in the six- to 12-year age group, and handicaps about 15 percent of all grade school children.

Dyslexia may stem from a variety of physical ailments or combinations of them — glandular imbalance, heart disease, eye or ear trouble —

or from a deep-seated psychological disturbance that blocks a child's ability to learn. It has little or nothing to do with intelligence and is usually curable.[11]

John Dewey must have smiled from his grave. He knew using images and pictures to teach reading would create confusion in the minds of children. As a result, reading would become a hurdle over which many students would never jump.

In Philadelphia, "less than half of the city's 215,000 students have mastered basic reading skills."[12]

**Reading became a hurdle over which
many students would never jump.**

Samuel Blumenfeld researched the origin of "look-say" and discovered it was invented by Thomas H. Gallaudet, a teacher who worked with the deaf. Since the deaf could not hear sound, Gallaudet devised the sight method. To teach the word CAT, he would hold up a picture of a cat. This technique was quite effective and enabled the deaf to read — although with some limitations.

Thinking this method could be effective with normal children, Gallaudet created a little primer called *The Mother's Primer,* and published it in 1837. The Boston primary schools adopted the method "on an experimental basis" and used it until 1844, when, after seven years, the first batch of experimental students were arriving in Boston's upper grades.

At that point, the teachers rebelled and wrote a scathing critique of the "look-say" approach, noting that, "These kids aren't learning to read by this method of teaching."[13]

Maybe that's what America needs today — a teachers' rebellion.

A NEW BREED OF EDUCATORS

By the turn of the century, educators had forgotten about the Boston experiment, and the Progressives were in charge of American education.

Who belonged to this new breed of educators? Blumenfeld describes them:

> These were members of the Protestant academic elite who no longer believed in the religion of their fathers. These men now put their faith in science, evolution, and psychology. Science explained the material world, and evolution explained the origin of living matter. Psychology now permitted these educators to study the human mind and the human personality scientifically, like an animal. Of course it also provided them with scientific methods of controlling human behavior. They had it all. They said, "We don't need religion. We have all the tools we need."[14]

As socialists, these men — like the Unitarians — no longer believed in the biblical explanation for the cause of evil. Instead of accepting the fact that man's sinful nature and innate depravity requires God's forgiveness and His salvation, they decided that evil resulted from outside sources like ignorance, poverty, and social injustice.

"Social injustice" became their battle cry and the capitalist system their perceived enemy. To rally the troops they carried the banner of hatred and shouted, "Look at all the inequities!"

Blumenfeld describes their mission:

> They decided if they got rid of capitalism, individualism and religion, and replaced them with socialism, collectivism, and atheism or humanism, then again we could have this perfect society. We could have this Utopia. These were the thoughts of these educators in the 1880s and 1890s.[15]

At that point, the battle for America's children began. Strategies were plotted and battle plans devised to capture the hearts and minds of future generations.

John Dewey, probably the chief social philosopher of this new group of Progressives, pinpointed the greatest threat to their socialistic goals: "the individualistic belief system." As he analyzed the power behind this threat, he asked: What sustains individualism? What sustains religion? What is the key?

Dewey discovered the answer. It was "high literacy" and the "emphasis on language learning."

Blumenfeld explains the threat behind these phrases:

> Because high literacy produced people with independent intelligence who can stand on their own two feet and think for themselves. They didn't need the collective, they didn't need the group, they could find truth for themselves. Also, high literacy permitted children to be able to read the Bible.[16]

The enemies of God hate the Bible. It is impossible for them to accept the Bible as truth, and at the same time build their own kingdoms. Such has been the case since the Garden of Eden and the Tower of Babel.

High literacy sustains individualism and religion, two enemies of socialism.

Dewey and his friends were simply another group of rebels determined to do things their way. What was the greatest obstacle on their road to nowhere? America's Christian heritage of biblical instruction and its emphasis on teaching children to read God's Word at an early age.

As a result, "language study" — not of foreign languages but of English — became Dewey's target. In 1898, he laid out his plan to eliminate the study of English in the early grades:

It is almost an unquestioned assumption of educational theory and practice both that the first three years of a child's school life shall be mainly taken up with learning to read and write his own language. . . . It does not follow, however, that because this course was once wise, it is so any longer. My proposition is that conditions have undergone such a radical change that the time has come for a thorough-going examination of the emphasis put upon linguistic work in elementary instruction.[17]

Blumenfeld summarized Dewey's plan:

- De-emphasize the development of the academic, the linguistic, and the intellectual skills.
- Emphasize the development of social skills, beliefs, attitudes, morality, and values.
- Create a school system that would produce little socialists.
- Reform the entire educational system.
- Get rid of the emphasis on literacy.
- Emphasize the affective domain — the area that deals with emotions, feelings, and values.
- Lower the literacy level by using the "look-say" method.[18]

268 *Aim for the Children*

Their objective was clear: Keep America's children down at a level where they could be easily led and less resistant to control. Psychological manipulation was their ultimate goal and absolutely critical to the success of their socialist revolution.

HALF-BAKED "WHOLE LANGUAGE"

If your child attends public school, you have probably heard the term "whole language" tossed around. Sounds good, doesn't it? Who wouldn't want their child to be able to incorporate all aspects of reading, writing, and spelling into useful and effective forms of communication?

Whole language is a prescription for failure.

But is that really what educators hope to accomplish? Not according to those who promote the "whole language" method in the book, *Whole Language: What's the Difference?* In their usual, high-minded — and purposely confusing — manner the authors write: "From a whole language perspective, reading is a process of generating a hypothesis in a meaning-making transaction, in a socio-historical context."

Did you get that? Neither did I. They do go on to explain, but we still have to read between the lines of their jargon:

As a transactional process, reading is not a matter of getting the meaning from text, as if that meaning were in the text itself, waiting to be decoded by the reader. Rather reading is a matter of readers using the clues print provides and the knowledge they bring with them to construct a unique interpretation.[19]

We need Professor Blumenfeld to help us translate this paragraph. He says, "This view of reading implies that there was no single correct meaning for a given text, only plausible meanings."

In other words, Blumenfeld notes, they tell students, "You interpret what it is. First of all, we're not going to read phonetically, so you are going to have to look at each one of these words to decide what they mean, and you can create your own meaning."

Rather than viewing reading as knowing the words, reading is seen as a process of "creating meanings." Words no longer have uniform dictionary meanings, rather, they have "meaning potentials" and the "capacity to communicate multiple meanings," according to the whole language brigade.

Create your own meaning of words? If that's the case, why bother to read? Could that be the real objective? First, they make reading so hard that kids will give up; then teachers tell them, "The words don't matter anyway; you can make up your own meanings."

Why then do we need authors?

Blumenfeld answers, "If the reader is going to create the meaning, forget about the authors. You wonder why authors are so careful about their selection of words. They want to be understood. They want to be read as they wrote the piece. They don't want somebody to edit what they wrote. They want the person to understand what they are saying."[20]

Whole language goes far beyond the "look-say" method and the Dick and Jane method, which at least pretended to teach kids to read. The goal was still to make students good readers.

Whole language encourages students to "create their own meaning" for words as they read.

Whole language proponents have something entirely different in mind, as they explain in their own words: "Whole language represents a major shift in thinking about the reading process."

This process, however, is a prescription for failure because it confuses and frustrates young children who are told to guess or substitute words using "configuration clues." Although a smattering of phonics is taught, Blumenfeld notes educators do this "in order to create the cognitive confusion," resulting in an inability to read.

No wonder America has such a high rate of functional illiterates today.

What is the only cure for functional illiteracy? "Intensive systemic phonics," is Blumenfeld's answer.

Is your child at risk for becoming illiterate? Blumenfeld thinks so: "If your child is in public school today, the chances of that child becoming dyslexic or functionally illiterate are very high. I would say that in some places it's 60 to 75 percent."

INVENTED SPELLING

Some of us have been doing this all wrong, pouring over the dictionary and thesaurus and grammar books, searching for the right word, agonizing over every sentence. Think of the time we could have saved, creating our own words and inventing our own spelling. How free we might have been, unloosed from the shackles of correct spelling and proper syntax. After all, the mood of the moment is to question authority.

But don't take it from me; let an educator speak. Sandra Wilde of the University of Nevada writes on the subject of "invented spelling" — a new spelling curriculum that shifts from "a focus on error to a focus on creation."

Professor Wilde writes that "the usual view of spelling is either right or wrong." She calls this archaic since "spelling text books do not, for the most part, see students as individuals."

Let me summarize her views:

■ Children should be "encouraged to invent their own spellings . . . they will be independent spellers from the start."

■ Teachers should rarely tell students "how to spell a word."

■ Students should be encouraged to "try different spellings to see how they look, discuss possible spellings with their peers."

■ Teaching spelling short-circuits the "creative, intellectual process."

■ American students are "rotten spellers, and their grammatical errors are often an embarrassment."[21]

Wilde suggests that teachers allow students to spell any way they please. Who cares if no one else can read what kids write? Low grades and red markers produce low self-esteem, and we can't have that!

We've thrown out the dictionary to boost a student's creativity and self-esteem!

Wilde goes on to say that spelling words correctly is only a "question of etiquette" and that "everyone needs to relax a bit more about spelling."

I leave it to your imagination to wonder at the chaos such an approach would create. But, then, isn't that exactly the objective of a social revolution?

REDEFINED LITERACY

In the early 1980s, a Minnesota school district defined the literate person as "one who has developed a feeling of self-worth" and "respects other people and cultures" and has "a desire for learning." The literate person is "one who continues to seek knowledge, to increase personal skills and the quality of relations with others, and to fulfill individual potential."[22]

Did you notice they didn't mention the words "read" or "write"?

Charles J. Sykes, in his book, *Dumbing Down Our Kids,* explains the reason: "Another response of educationists to the decline of literacy has been to simply change the definition of literacy. A literate person is no longer someone who has mastered the grammar, usage, and diction of language."[23]

**Have you noticed the new definition
for literacy doesn't include
reading and writing?**

Why the need to redefine literacy? Because educators can no longer hide the fact that, according to Sykes, "the number of functional illiterate Americans is in the tens of millions" and "SAT verbal scores have reached historic lows."

Sykes notes other embarrassing statistics from a 1994 report by the Educational Testing Service:

▪ Half of the nation's college graduates could not read a bus schedule.

▪ Only 42 percent could summarize an argument presented in a newspaper article.

▪ Only 35 percent of the college graduates were able to consistently write a brief letter about a billing error.[24]

Another study found that American businesses lose "nearly 40 billion dollars in revenue each year because of the low level of their employees' literacy and the added time needed to train and retrain workers for new technologies."

Sykes includes this example: "Recently, the Stone Savannah River Pulp and Paper Corporation had to spend $200,000 to train workers to use computers after managers found that workers lacked the reading skills needed to operate the equipment."[25]

The problem wasn't dyslexia or diminished intelligence. The problem was the lack of "reading skills" that 12 years of schooling failed to provide.

In 1987, California abandoned phonetic instruction and embraced a "literature-based" approach to reading. Instead of learning the rules and skills needed to "sound out" words for themselves, kids were taught to read by experiencing "the wonders of literature," Sykes informs us.

Six years later, in 1993, a national reading survey conducted by the Educational Testing Service found that California fourth graders ranked 49 out of the 50 states — "dead last in their reading abilities compared with students throughout the country."

How did educators explain this major blunder?

"There's a lot of evidence that first graders who do not get instruction in phonics fail to read adequately," said Robert E. Slavin of Johns Hopkins University's Center. "It's possible that the kids in the last several years were not taught word attack skills adequately."[26]

I recall the television station that identified itself each night at 10 o'clock, then asked: "Do you know where your children are?"

How about your kids? Where are they now? Are they floating around in elementary school, struggling to read anything more challenging than a comic book? If so, it may be time for a reality check. The last thing you want is to wake up on graduation day and find your youngsters — not on the road to the future — but on the road to nowhere.

CHAPTER ELEVEN

A World Within the World

"We've lost," the young man said.

"Lost what?" I asked.

"The culture," he replied. "We've lost the culture."

I knew him to be a bright young man — not given to careless, intemperate remarks — neither negative temperamentally nor consumed by pessimistic sentiments, certainly no cynic. Still, it was his reasoned, honest assessment of our national condition.

He must be reading the same newspapers as Robert Bork, who remarks, "Large chunks of the moral life of the United States, major features of its culture, have disappeared altogether, and more are in the process of extinction."[1]

The disappearance is doubly dangerous if we get used to it. The Bible warns that the love of good people wanes when evil abounds. The temptation to apathy is ever present. "With each new evidence of deterioration," Bork notes, "we lament for a moment, and then become accustomed to it."[2]

But this is no time to throw in the towel. A salient characteristic of the Christian faith is the belief that a better day may dawn. A wise man said, "The mercies of the Lord are new every morning."

During his first visit to Great Britain, young Billy Graham was invited to visit Winston Churchill. The American evangelist and the war-time prime minister chatted amiably for a few minutes, then discussed some troubling developments in the world. Churchill raised the issue of crime and noted how passively violence is accepted. Then he leaned across the table and asked, "Young man, do you have any hope?"

This book has become a rather dreary recitation of bad news. By the third or fourth chapter, you may have abandoned any hope of better schools, saner teachers, smarter students, or safer streets.

After a storm uproots the trees, breaks the windows, rips the roof off the house, and scares everybody half to death, one assesses the damage, counts the cost of repairs, takes heart, and goes to work.

I HAVE AN IDEA

We have at some length assessed the damage done to our culture by a rampant atheism and secularism. It is time now to take heart and begin the task of repairing the breach. What can be done?

An idea has been percolating in my mind for some time. Mentioned briefly in an earlier chapter, it has to do with the novel concept of living radically — of throwing caution to the winds and launching a building program that would bring heaven to our side and secure the encouragement and assistance of good people once they've caught the vision.

I propose the building of . . . a subculture within the framework of a pagan system.

Given the minimal impact the church is making in our society, I have wondered why the tens of millions of professing Christians in America are doing so little to heal the nation. What a British Catholic said at mid-century of his church's influence in Britain may be said about evangelicals in America: "On the one hand, there is the enormous growth, and on the other, there is the almost complete lack of influence."

Christianity has flourished in recent years; church attendance has exploded. Radio and television have succeeded in putting Jesus on Main Street, but in too many cases the children, even those raised in "Christian" homes, drift away, lose interest, and become indifferent — if not hostile — to the gospel.

Has the gospel failed? Or have we failed to try it? Has the Word of God been rendered ineffectual, or have we annulled it by a superficial handling of its commands?

Straight answers are required and direct action needed if we are to stop the trend toward a totally secular society unhinged from morality, civility, and common decency. Optimism and hopefulness are gifts to the believer. As we affirm our faith in the goodness of God, let us search for ways to live victoriously in troubled times, knowing that as long as God's people are present, there is hope.

I propose the building of a new world. Not a "New World Order," but a new world, a subculture within the framework of a pagan system.

This idea of constructing "a world within the world" was triggered by a visit to a family in the Midwest. We were invited to dinner and welcomed by the parents and seven children, ranging in age from one to 17.

Several things attracted my attention about this family. The children stood as we came in — the older ones extending a hand of welcome. We sat down to eat a home-cooked meal served at a long table with mother at one end, father at the other, and the guests in between. No raucous music emanated from a bedroom somewhere, to which sullen youngsters had come and to which they couldn't wait to return.

These children were not bored by adults. We ate, talked, laughed, shared; no one was in a hurry to leave. The older children helped the younger. We all enjoyed the food and fellowship — and each other.

I knew I had to have a long visit with these parents, so when I returned home, I called them and made some interesting discoveries. It began eight years ago, shortly after the parents found Christ. As they searched the Scriptures, they uncovered worn principles once known to most American families.

A BLESSING NOT A BURDEN

First of all, the parents discovered children are a blessing not a burden!

"Behold, children are a heritage from the Lord," the Bible says. "The fruit of the womb is His reward. Like arrows in the hand of a warrior, so are the children of one's youth. Happy is the man who has his quiver full of them; They shall not be ashamed, but shall speak with their enemies in the gate" (Psalm 127:3-5).

How totally different has been the attitude fostered among us for a generation. Much of education, state welfare, child care programs, government "snoopervision," the feminist movement — all have contributed to the notion that children are a liability.

We have created a cultural climate in America that wars against the family and the home. "The mother at home is continually intimidated and devalued by others," one mother commented. "I find myself vacillating and wondering about my worth due to the pressures placed on me by the world's value system."

Father Patrick W. Egan, writing in *Pastoral Renewal*, identifies the cause of much of our social disintegration:

American parents spend considerably less time with their children than parents in almost any other nation in the world. A home in which both parents are available to the child emotionally as well as physically has become, in some areas of our society, the exception rather than the rule — and I refer not only to the disadvantaged home where the father is missing and the mother works, but also to even the most affluent homes.

A man and a woman ought to be free to become whatever they choose. If, however, they choose to be parents — to have a child — then they must be willing to spend time with that child and to give him or her priority over social, career, and other ambitions. They must find pleasure in the child. Nothing contributes more to a positive self-image in a child than the repeated experience that his presence brings pleasure to his parents.

Many young parents today resent children because children interfere with their "fulfillment." We in the "me generation" need to hear a little less about self-fulfillment and a little more about self-denial. Perhaps denial and sacrificial love is the ultimate key to fulfillment.[3]

Wendy Dreskin was a childcare provider until she discovered the stress put on children enduring full-day daycare. She now spends her time helping parents develop other options.

She tells of a news interview in which "daycare graduates" talked about their experiences. No one seemed to notice what one little boy said, but it struck a note with Dreskin: "I think daycare is a good thing because it frees parents from the burden of children."

Dreskin comments, "Here is a *child* saying that children are a burden and an encumbrance to our society."[4]

When politicians clamor for state-sanctioned day-care centers, parents must question if they really want "the government — which gave us the welfare system, which destroyed a generation and paved the road to hell in America's inner cities" to take care of their small children.

Children are a heritage from the Lord, and parents are entrusted with their care. The great battle in the classrooms of our schools and halls of our legislatures centers around the question: Who owns the children?

WHOSE CHILDREN ARE THEY?

Don't ask Dan Rather who owns the children. Apparently he thinks we should take a cue from the Marxists.

On February 21, 1988, during a segment on the CBS *Evening News* promoting federal government daycare, Rather said, "Whatever else the Soviet Union does, it takes care of its children. Daycare is provided for all children from two months of age."

A visit to the former Soviet Union would reveal the mindlessness of that remark. The tragedy that ensues when the state assumes sovereignty over human life from the cradle to the grave is not pleasant to behold. One must step with a heavy heart over the broken pieces of a system from which God has been dismissed and freedom stifled.

Americans are taking a cue from the wrong people.

As early as 1901, the Supreme Court of Indiana upheld a compulsory education law by arrogantly declaring, "The natural rights of a parent to the custody and control of his children are subordinate to the power of the state."

President Clinton has signed a new international treaty called, "The United Nations Convention of the Rights of the Child." If this treaty is ratified by the U.S. Senate, children would have the rights to freedom of association, freedom of peaceful assembly, and privacy. Parents would not be able to prevent their children from watching pornography on the Internet, if that's what the kids choose to do.

Much of the assault against children takes place in America's public school system. According to a *Heritage Foundation Issue Bulletin,* incidents like the following happen on a regular basis:[5]

■ In Pennsylvania, parents were outraged to learn that school authorities had ordered gynecological examinations of their sixth grade daughters without permission from parents. Many of the children were so terrified by the experience that several tried to escape out the windows.

■ In Massachusetts, parents filed a lawsuit to stop schools from dispensing condoms in restroom vending machines. The state Supreme Court ruled against the parents.

■ In Maryland, Montgomery County, parents expressed their outrage over pro-homosexual material in the public school curriculum. The school board decided to disregard their concern and go ahead with the curriculum. The officials would not allow their students to "opt out" of the sexual education classes.

■ In Michigan, parents of an eight-year-old boy were horrified to learn that their son had been subjected to psychotherapeutic counseling by an untrained education bureaucrat over their objections. The young child was later diagnosed as having suffered severe emotional trauma as a direct result of the misguided counseling.

■ In Washington state, the parents of an eighth grade girl grounded her because she intended to smoke marijuana and sleep with her boyfriend. The girl asked a local child welfare agency to place her somewhere else. The welfare agency agreed and removed the girl from her home, over the objections of her parents (who were never accused of any kind of abuse).

"Not so long ago," Dana Mack writes in *The Assault on Parenthood: How Our Culture Undermines the*

Family, "parents were looked upon as repositories of wisdom and rectitude, and they were the unchallenged custodians of their children's welfare. That is no longer the case. . . . Bookstores are flooded with tomes portraying parents as lethal to children and conveying the impression that child mistreatment is a ubiquitous social malaise."[6]

Who are the culprits? According to author Patricia Love, parents are. She writes that "parents who educate their children at home, spend time with their children in the pursuit of common interests and hobbies, and especially parents who take their children into the parental bed for cuddles" are over-involved.

I thought being *uninvolved* was the problem. Now loving, caring, concerned parents are labeled as "over-involved"?

Raymond S. Moore, an authority on home education, contradicts Ms. Love's statement when he notes: "No documented evidence appears . . . of a delinquent who has been raised exclusively by his parents."[7]

PARENTS AS TEACHERS

My friends in the Midwest discovered that the Bible has a great deal to say about parents, children, the home, and other practical issues. They were surprised to find how insistently God commands parents to teach their children.

Deuteronomy 6:1-9 records Moses' words to the nation of Israel:

"Now this is the commandment, and these are the statutes and judgments which the Lord your God has commanded to teach you, that you may observe them in the land which you are crossing over to possess, that you may fear the Lord your God, to keep all His statutes and His commandments which I command you, you and your son and your grandson, all the days of your life, and that your days may be prolonged. Therefore hear, O Israel, and be careful to observe it, that it may be well with you, and that you may multiply greatly as the Lord God of your fathers has promised you — 'a land flowing with milk and honey.'

"Hear, O Israel: The Lord our God, the Lord is one! You shall love the Lord your God with all your heart, with all your soul, and with all your might. And these words which I command you today shall be in your heart; you shall teach them diligently to your children, and shall talk of them when you sit in your house, when you walk by the way, when you lie down, and when you rise up. You shall bind them as a sign on your hand, and they shall be as frontlets between your eyes. You shall write them on the doorposts of your house and on your gates."

The parents asked God to forgive them for not taking seriously their responsibility and then asked their children to forgive them for disobeying the Word of God by not teaching them when they "lie down" and when they "rise up."

How can we do that, they asked, if our children are under the influence of others six to eight hours a day?

For these parents, the answer was home schooling.

HOME SCHOOLING'S SECRET OF SUCCESS

Did you know that 1.2 million school-age children are home schooled in America? This is more students than are enrolled in New Jersey, the state with the tenth largest school enrollment.

Also, there are more home schoolers nationally than there are public school students in Arkansas, Delaware, Hawaii, Montana, North Dakota, South Dakota, Rhode Island, Vermont, and Wyoming combined![8]

How are these students doing academically compared to public school students?

Michael Farris, president of the Home School Legal Defense Association in Purcellville, Virginia, provides some interesting statistics:[9]

■ Home school students score significantly higher on standardized achievement tests than their public-school counterparts.

■ Home-schooled ethnic minorities and whites both score on average in the 87th percentile on reading tests.

"Those who believe that government regulation is essential for success would do well to look at the cold, hard numbers that prove otherwise," notes Farris.

What does it cost to home school a child? About $546 per year. Compare that to the average $5,325 price tag to educate each pupil in America's public schools.

Home schools don't have any expensive facilities to maintain, skeptics argue. True, but both figures cited above "exclude the capital costs of the building in which each child is taught," according to Farris.

Most parents aren't qualified to teach their kids — at least that's what many critics like to think.

Once again Michael Farris has the facts, which indicate that parents' qualifications have little to do with student success:[10]

■ There is no significant statistical difference in student test scores between those taught by a parent who is or has been a certified teacher and those whose parents were never certified.

■ There is no significant statistical difference in student test scores between those taught by parents with a college degree, and students taught by those who have never attended college.

- Students taught by parents who have not finished high school score 30 percentiles higher than students in the public schools.

What is the secret of the success of the modern home-schooling movement? Two "old-fashioned concepts: hard work and parental involvement lead to the best individual academic achievement," notes Farris.

JUMPING THE GENERATION GAP

Ideas crystalized in my mind as I observed the parents and children of this Midwestern family, working and playing together — sharing their studies and a variety of experiences.

In such a loving and supportive environment, the issue of peer pressure becomes a moot point. After all, what is peer pressure? Isn't it the pressure that compels a young person to act in a certain way — often not in his own self-interest but to please his peers?

Age segregation leads to peer pressure and widens the generation gap.

How about the "generation gap" and all the heartache it causes? Is it necessary that a child be estranged from his parents in order to experience the adventure of youth?

What did H. L. Menken mean when he said that college is a place you send your son to learn to hate his father?

I am convinced that the age segregation we impose upon our young is the culprit leading to peer pressure and the widening of the generation gap. I know of no other culture that engages in such a practice as extensively as Americans do.

Even in church we break up the families, sending some members here and others there. Family night in most churches is anything but "family" night!

I wonder about the phenomenon repeated weekly in churches large and small. Just before the sermon, the children are dismissed. From every quarter of the auditorium they scramble for the exits, followed by teenagers and adults who provide the graded lessons.

Does this practice not suggest that preliminary remarks, singing, special music, announcements, receiving the offering are more important than the preaching? It is little wonder that in too many churches, by the age of 13, the kids are gone — not only from the sanctuary but from the church itself.

I am not minimizing the importance and value of quality children's programs, but is there not some benefit in permitting the children to hear the gospel preached in the "big church" at least on occasion? They may not catch each word or understand every point, but youngsters are not stupid. At least once in a while it might be profitable to have them sit and listen to something not immediately intelligible but which leaves them with a sense of God.

The most important spiritual lessons of my life were learned — "caught" — in the earliest years. To watch Mother and Father and other adults worship — to see their tears and hear their prayers — made an impact on me that endures until this day.

WHO NEEDS PEER PRESSURE?

Born in the mid-1950s, the idea of a "youth culture" resulted in the first teenage generation with its own music — fed and sustained primarily by rock-and-roll.

Someone has pointed out that the word *adolescent* entered our language less than 100 years ago. Until that time, no word was needed to describe the state between puberty and adulthood. Young men and women helped out at home, learned a trade, and were expected to begin working with their fathers or in a profession. The idea of 18 being the magic age when a boy becomes a man was ridiculous in a time when every able-bodied person was expected to carry his weight.

Families worked, played, and learned together. Even if children attended local schools, social gatherings of young people were few and far between. The home and farm or family business occupied the remaining hours, leaving little idle time.

I'm not advocating a return to the "horse and buggy" days, but somewhere along the rush to "progress," America let go of her children's hands and lost them in the hustle and bustle. Suddenly, youth had their own wild culture, and parents were left dazed and confused by the behavior of the stranger now living down the hall.

In the words of social historian Joseph Kett, "Adolescence was essentially a conception of behavior imposed on youth, rather than an empirical assessment of the way in which young people actually behaved."

After all, what do you get when you isolate thirty 15-year-olds in classes six to eight hours a day? No wonder they come home treating their parents like "one of the boys." Add to that an educational system that is dismissive of parents anyway, and you have a problem that will destroy any hope for a pleasant homelife.

Age segregation naturally lends itself to peer pressure and intimidation. The home schooling alternative reduces peer pressure and allows kids to be themselves in a loving, nurturing family environment.

TOO MUCH TOO SOON

Maybe we shouldn't be so quick to hand little five-year-old Johnny and Susie over to the state where they are suddenly at the mercy of strange children.

Let's face it, the attitude in most school environments is "every man for himself." Teachers have little time to defend weaker children from mean-spirited predators, and administrators are reluctant to punish kids who pick on others.

Columnist Arianna Huffington notes that in public schools nationwide, "160,000 students miss school daily because of intimidation or fear of bodily harm."[11]

During a recent Senate hearing on the need for school vouchers, a Cleveland mother testified that her eight-year-old daughter, while enrolled in public schools, "was hit, kicked, punched, and called names by other students."

As a result, Ms. Huffington notes, the girl was doing poorly in all subjects, cried uncontrollably at school, and considered by teachers to be a behavior problem in need of counseling. Through a scholarship program the girl was transferred to a better school where her grades dramatically improved and the "behavior problem" miraculously disappeared.

Aside from the emotional adjustment of going to school, young children must suddenly compete with dozens of other children for the attention of the lone adult teacher. This is one reason many parents decide to teach their youngsters themselves. Not only are young children taught in the safe and familiar home setting but they have the full attention of mom (or dad) as their teacher.

Could it be that rushing young children out of the home and into confined classrooms for long hours every day may do more harm than good? Every child is unique. Some children love the classroom environment and quickly catch on to the routine. Others are merely distracted and unable to focus in a large group.

Kids need more time to be kids. It's no secret that little boys especially seem to have trouble adjusting to a structured environment. Maybe that's because God created them to be out climbing trees and catching minnows.

Home schooled children have the world as their classroom. They may plant a garden in the backyard as part of a science project or visit the zoo to study animals. Family vacation could be a tour of the Civil War battlefields.

Is this a dangerous idea? The wholesome Christian family, living and learning together, somewhat protected from harsh winds of a world system that militates against righteousness?

Educational elitists think so. The NEA fights it tooth and nail. Is it because they love your children? Or because it impinges on their authority, erodes their support — your tax dollars — and restricts their power?

"GET YOUR KIDS OUT!"

Why does home schooling work? Because it focuses on the individual child.

"Public school reformers are constantly scheming with new ideas for all children. Such programs, like the federal government's Goals 2000, invariably lead to one-size-fits-all mediocrity," writes Farris. "Programs that allow each child to maximize his or her own individual abilities lead to success."

Then why don't public schools also adopt the "each child" theory? Good question.

There's only one problem: Teaching for the child's sake has never been the goal of modern educators. Since Horace Mann and John Dewey, the objective has always been one of social control. That's why unless there is a radical turning away from public education by parents, America's public school system will never change.

Social control — and not teaching for the child's sake — has been the goal of modern educators.

Not everyone will agree with Samuel Bloomenfeld when he suggests that Christians get their kids out of public schools before its too late:

If you want to reclaim America for Christ, there is the short way and there's the long way. The short way is for you to get your kids out of the public schools. If Christians in this country, most of whom put their kids in public schools, withdrew their kids from the public schools today, we would deprive all those psychologists, counselors, and change-agents, all of those people who are undermining our system, of what they need — the children. They would have all the empty buildings, and we would stop cold the entire process of turning this country into a socialist, fascist society. You could do it, but you've got to get your kids out. If not, it's going to take 10, 20 years, and there will be a lot of causalities. A lot of damage will be done.[12]

The quality of public schools, of course, varies from place to place, with some pockets of excellence to be found. Home schooling will not fit the needs of every family, but there are alternatives. In certain areas, private Christian schools are available, and many parochial schools offer an excellent academic education. In other cases, parents are banding together, pooling their skills, and forming their own schools.

Whatever course one chooses, the spiritual as well as intellectual welfare of our children should be considered.

A PECULIAR PEOPLE

At times, good people are required to make tough decisions. And it takes courage to stand alone. "How glorious it is — and how painful — to be an exception," someone once said.

When God implemented His plan of redemption, the first thing He did was call a man — Abraham. Called to build a family and a nation, isolated in a narrow strip of land, this family was to be a *peculiar* people, that is, a people for God's own possession.

They were to be different. They had their own dietary laws and manner of dress; their worship was distinct. They were separated from the other nations and were to be a separate people.

They were isolated in order to be taught by God to equip them to bring the light to the Gentiles. They never fully realized that their isolation, their solitary dwelling, was not an end in itself. God's purpose was to teach them "line upon line" in order to prepare them for evangelism.

What does that have to do with us? Is God calling us to build a world within the world — not as an end in itself, but to prepare us to evangelize our towns and cities, and to impact the culture?

Consider the alternative. How will we achieve God's purpose for us as "a peculiar people" if we continue tossing our little ones to the wolves, allowing those who do not share our beliefs and values to train them?

Before our children can go out to fight the Lord's battles, they must be trained and developed into mighty warriors who can stand against the onslaught of a wicked society.

What can we do? Permit me to make a few challenging recommendations.

TAKE YOUR FAITH SERIOUSLY

Radical Christian living begins by taking our faith seriously.

Jesus said, "You shall love the Lord your God with all your heart, with all your soul, and with all your mind." Superficial Christianity is the curse of the church.

Mark Noll, McManis professor of Christian Thought at Wheaton College, writes, "The scandal of the evangelical mind is that there is not much of an evangelical mind."

He laments the undisciplined and shabby response to the call of Christ stated above. "Despite dynamic success at a popular level," he writes, "modern American evangelicals have failed notably in sustaining serious intellectual life. They have nourished millions of believers in the simple verities of the gospel, but have largely abandoned the universities, the arts, and other realms of 'high' culture."[13]

It is nothing short of scandalous to counsel seekers at an altar of prayer to disengage mentally — to "let go and let God." The pursuit of God requires as much diligence as the pursuit of the law or the study of languages.

"Evangelicals have been deeply sinful in being anti-intellectual ever since the 1820s and 1830s," Os Guinness, Senior Fellow with the Trinity Forum, writes. He goes on to say:

For the longest time, we didn't pay the cultural price for that because we had the numbers, the social zeal, and the spiritual passion for the gospel. But we are beginning to pay the cultural price. And you can see today most evangelicals simply don't think. For example, there has been no serious evangelical public philosophy in this century. It has always been a sin not to love the Lord our God with our minds as well as our hearts and souls. We have excused this with a degree of pietism and pretending that this is something other than what it is — that is, sin. Evangelicals need to repent of their refusal to think Christianly and to develop the mind of Christ.[14]

Serious people will not be attracted to a faith that is shallow and cheap. It is too late in the day for a gospel that is heavy on noise and motion but short on substance and commitment.

**The pursuit of God requires as much
diligence as the pursuit of the law
or the study of languages.**

Charles Malik warned in his address at the Billy Graham Center, "The problem is not only to win souls but to save minds. If you win the whole world and lose the mind of the world, you will soon discover you have not won the world. Indeed, it may turn out you have actually lost the world."

GIVE ATTENTION TO READING

To "save the mind" and "win the world" requires application. Reading is a good place to begin.

I grew up in a small house at the end of First Avenue. There were five boys and one girl together with Mother and Father in five rooms where we ate, slept, laughed, played, worked, fought, and prayed together.

By today's standards, we were poor — although it never occurred to us at the time. We grew up without television or computers and never saw a big city newspaper. But we had books. And those books fired the imagination and enabled us to fly the skies and travel the seas.

I remember the set of missionary biographies. John G. Paton introduced us to the South Seas. We all wanted to be missionaries when we read the story of David Livingstone, who opened Africa to the gospel — and Adoniram Judson, the first American to go to a foreign field.

We were inspired by the testimony of William Carey, the shoemaker, who worked under a large map of the world on his wall. Always engaged in evangelism, Carey prayed for those countries while he made and mended shoes.

When he intensified his evangelistic efforts, a friend said, "I fear you are neglecting your business for your ministry."

Carey's prompt reply was, "Neglect my business? My business, sir, is to extend the kingdom of Christ. I only make and mend shoes to help pay expenses." He went to India as a missionary and made an impact that endures to this day.

An inspiring story that emphasizes the advantages of reading is told in the book, *Gifted Hands:*

Bennie, a black child, was the worst student in this fifth-grade class at Higgins Elementary School, where most students were white. He endured a mocking by classmates after scoring a perfect zero out of 30 on a math test. He was diagnosed as visually handicapped and got glasses. His grades rose from F's to D's.

Then Ben's mother turned off the television set. "From now on," she said, "you can watch no more that three programs a week." She pointed out that Ben could either waste time in front of the TV, or shut it off and be *on* it someday, but not both. She ordered him and his brother to read two books a week and give her a report on them. "Books are the key to success. The doors of the world are open to people who can read. And my boys are going to be successful in life. Bennie, you can do anything you set yourself to do."

Gradually, Ben's reluctant trips to the library turned into an exciting challenge and developed into a thirst for learning. By the time he entered the seventh grade, he was the top student in his class. He had overcome peer pressure, racial prejudice, and a very bad temper. During his teen years, he gave his life to the Lord. Then he received a scholarship to Yale University. Today, Dr. Benjamin Carson is the world-famous chief neurosurgeon of Johns Hopkins University. And, yes, he has appeared on television, just as his mother predicted.[15]

Our busy, nervous age militates against contemplation. Ideas and ideals, concepts and insights await the serious student. The great literature of the world holds undiscovered adventures, unsung music, unrealized dreams; and wise parents and teachers will encourage the young by precept and example to develop a taste for reading.

FIND NEW HEROES

Good books introduce children — and adults — to persons worthy of emulation. That's important because our choice of heroes provides an index to our character. Someone once said a nation's heroes tell us more about the nation than about its heroes.

"We can't all be heroes," Will Rogers once noted. "Somebody has to sit on the curb and clap as they go by."

There's little danger today of too many heroes; the country is full of hand clappers sitting on the curb. Not only is there a shortage of role models, but those we do have diminish rather than elevate and inspire: Like the rising star Melissa Joan Hart, who counsels aspiring actors, "Have no shame. If there's a role that calls for being corny or goofy, no matter how stupid it feels, you've got to go for it."

No matter how vulgar or profane, rock stars, rap artists, and movie idols are applauded by adoring fans. Even some Christians show little discretion when it comes to heroes and ignore the biblical principle: "He who walks with wise men shall be wise, but the companion of fools will be destroyed" (Prov. 13:20).

"For many people, life has lost its dimensions," Dr. Karl Menninger observes. "The heights and depths are gone, and life has become flat and dull and cheap and frivolous."[16]

Dr. J. Alan Peterson notes the discrepancies in American society:

The puzzle is why so many people live so badly. Not so wickedly, but so inanely. Not so cruelly, but so stupidly. There is little to admire and less to imitate in the people who are prominent in our culture. We have celebrities but not saints. Famous entertainers amuse a nation of bored insomniacs. Infamous criminals act out the aggressions of timid conformists. Petulant and spoiled athletes play games vicariously for lazy and apathetic spectators. People, aimless and bored, amuse themselves with trivia and trash. Neither the adventure of goodness nor the pursuits of righteousness get headlines.[17]

"Modern man is 'a bleak business,'" says Tom Howard. "To our chagrin, we discover that the declaration of autonomy has issued not in a race of free, masterly men, but rather in a race that can be described by its poets and dramatists only as bored, vexed, frantic, embittered, and sniffling."[18]

Dr. Peterson also notes,

No other culture has been as eager to reward either nonsense or wickedness. If, on the other hand, we look around for what it means to be a mature, whole, blessed person, we don't find much. These people are around, maybe as many of them as ever, but they aren't easy to pick out. No journalist interviews them. No talk show features them. They are not admired. They are not looked up to. They do not set trends. There is no cash value in them. No Oscars are given for integrity. At year's end, no one compiles a list of the ten best-lived lives.[19]

That's why it takes some initiative on our part. Many of the finest minds in America today are Christians: Dr. C. Everett Koop, Robert Bork, Charles

Colson, Dr. Benjamin Nathanson, Carl F. H. Henry. Their writings will set a fire under any apathetic Christian.

And don't forget: The Bible is full of heroes.

GUARD THE HOME

Families who have taken a stand against America's culture of filth and retreated into their homes are accused of "isolating their children from the real world."

"Your kids will grow up ignorant of the larger world," such parents are told.

The apostle Paul has an answer for the critics: "I want you to be wise in what is good, and simple [innocent] concerning evil" (Romans 16:19).

The apostle Peter agreed: "I urge you, as aliens and strangers in the world, to abstain from sinful desires" (1 Peter 2:11, NIV).

Alexander Pope put it this way:

Vice is a monster of so frightful mien
As to be hated needs but to be seen;
Yet seen too oft, familiar with her face,
We first endure, then pity, then embrace.

It will not be easy to provide a safe and challenging environment for our children, but it can be done. E. Lonnie Melashenko recounts the efforts of one mother to steer her youngsters in the right direction:

A mother 25 years ago observed her two pre-schoolers sitting in front of the television watching "The Flintstones" and "I Love Lucy." For the first time, she noticed their trance-like stare and glazed eyes. "This is weird," she thought. "They don't look like that in normal life." So Marie Winn began to do research and ended up writing the book *The Plug-in Drug,* published in 1977.

Ten years later, she published *Unplugging the Plug-in Drug,* in which she gives the recipe for turning off the hypnotic tube and substituting various activities that stimulate the brain and cause it to develop the ability to think critically. Although her husband was an award-winning documentary filmmaker, the couple turned off the TV in their home. Today, son Steve is a professional violinist, and Mike is a journalist who published a book while still a teenager.[20]

As Christians, shouldn't we be setting the standard not only for moral purity but also for academic excellence and educational pursuits? The place to start is within the walls of our own homes.

GET INVOLVED. DO SOMETHING!

If the culture is lost, it was lost by default.

Until 100 years ago, every university president in America was a clergyman or a person trained by the

Church. Today, not one major university has a clergyman in the president's office.

Why? Because we failed to engage in the intellectual battles in the universities. We didn't encourage our children to enter law, the arts, to find their place in the lecture halls. We complained about a biased, left-leaning media but failed to train our young to be newspaper editors or television reporters.

**If the culture is lost,
it was lost by default.**

The Southern Baptist Convention decided to do something. For years, they watched warily as the Walt Disney Corporation sank deeper and deeper. Finally, weary after appeals for change went unheeded, the Convention voted with their pocketbooks to boycott the world of Mickey Mouse and Donald Duck. As a result, Southern Baptists were called bigots, homophobic, and unchristian-Christians. They were told the boycott was too broad; it will never work.

But "critics are missing something," Cal Thomas writes.

In an age when even some clergy are rushing to keep pace with the increasingly depraved culture, it's nice to see someone take a stand.

No one thought the young man standing in front of a tank in Tiananmen Square eight summers ago would be successful in deterring the Chinese army from firing its appointed rounds, but that image spoke to a world gone mushy about the power of one.

In each of these cases, the question was less about the effectiveness of the action than it was about the nobility, courage, and morality of the stand.

For years, William Wilberforce in the English Parliament stood alone in his opposition to Britain's involvement in the slave trade. He was mocked and told his position was futile. On his deathbed, he learned that Parliament had come around to his point of view.

David shamed his elders by taking on felling Goliath, who was said to be unbeatable. Statuary Hall in the U.S. Capitol is lined with marble memorials to men and women of courage who stood against what was popular, and upheld what was right and virtuous. America's Founders risked their lives and fortunes, but because they stood for principle against seemingly impossible odds, none lost his sacred honor.

It is that perceived loss of quality that produced the boycott vote by the Southern Baptist Convention. Its members may not be able to force Disney to change some of its policies or programming, but they're standing up for the principles. In what has become a gelded age, that may be enough.[21]

Some questioned the prudence of the plucky Baptists. The president of the Convention was interviewed after the vote. "Disney owns ABC, ESPN, and a variety of other industries. How can you avoid this?" he was asked.

"There were children before Walt Disney," he replied. In other words, who says we can't survive without Disney?

If the corner store sold poisoned candy, would you warn the neighborhood children? At some point the people of God will be forced to draw a line in the sand and make a stand. It may not be easy, but who said it would be?

Harriet Beecher Stowe was married to a preacher and teacher and raised a brood of children. Later she took to writing, and after some success as an author, her sister-in-law in Boston wrote to her saying, "Hattie, if I could use the pen as you can, I would write something that will make this whole nation feel what an accursed thing slavery is."

Harriet's husband, Calvin, thought little of the book. Her publisher was unimpressed, but the people loved it. "Within a week after publication," David McCullough, author of *Truman,* relates, "Ten thousand copies had been sold. The publisher had three power presses running 24 hours a day. In a year, sales in the United States came to more than 300,000."[22]

The book made publishing history right from the start. In England, where Mrs. Stowe had no copyright and therefore received no royalties, sales were even more stupendous. A million and a half copies were sold in about a year's time. The book appeared in 37 different languages.

"It is no longer permissible to those who can read not to have read it," wrote George Sand from France, who called the author a saint who had no talent, only genius.

The book was *Uncle Tom's Cabin.* Lincoln is supposed to have said as he shook Stowe's hand, "So this is the little woman who made this big war."

McCullough notes the importance of Mrs. Stowe's contribution:

There is a sweep and power to the narrative, and there are scenes that once read are not forgotten. What the book did at the time was to bring slavery out into the open and show it for what it was, in human terms. . . . No writer had done that before. Slavery had been argued over in the abstract, preached against as a moral issue, its evil whispered about in polite company. But the book made people at that time *feel* what slavery was about.[23]

Uncle Tom's Cabin became the catalyst to outlawing slavery.

Maybe a quiet housewife — or perhaps a student somewhere — will write a book or make a film to so stir the conscience of America that abortion — like slavery — will be abolished.

Do something! Don't just sit there and let others set the agenda.

We can no longer afford the luxury of living self-centered lives.

GIVE YOUR CHILDREN GOD

Recovery of our lost culture begins with God. "But seek first the kingdom of God. . . ." (Matthew 6:33). Denying this generation a spiritual foundation has led to tragic consequences. We can no longer afford the luxury of living self-centered lives.

I read of a speaker who gave a program in a school that asked him back a year later. On the way to the auditorium, the principal made one request: "Please don't mention God this time."

The speaker felt surprised because he had not openly mentioned his faith in Jesus. He had only generally referred to it.

"Okay," the speaker told the principal. "I'll make a deal with you. I will not mention Jesus, faith in God, or our need to lean on Him and go to Him for advice."

The principle began to smile until he heard the rest of the deal.

"I'll not mention God if you will promise me one thing."

"What's that?"

"That you will be there for these kids 100 percent of the time when they are hurting — that's 24 hours a day. Make certain your phone is never busy because I have taught kids that, if they go to God in prayer, He will never be too busy for them. Make sure that you tell the most unpopular kids in the school — the most unloved and the biggest trouble-makers — that you will be their best friend. You will never leave them and will always listen to them. I want you to visit them daily and be willing to die for them. If you do this, I will not mention God. I won't have to."

The principal got the message. "I tell you what I think we should do. You go ahead and do what you normally do. Don't alter your message one bit. Keep bringing God in here. Now I see why they appreciate you so much."[24]

Who else can do for our children what God can do? Let us encourage them to turn to Him.

CHANGE YOUR WAYS OR CHANGE YOUR NAME

David Mains tells a story that summarizes the challenge I have sought to present in this book:

A young man in the army of Alexander the Great had disgraced himself by running from the rabble. Normally this act of cowardice was punishable by death, but in a magnanimous moment of victory, Alexander listened to the pleas of an officer on behalf of the youth and excused him. The young man prostrated himself in shame and gratitude.

Alexander began to walk away, then turned, and almost as an afterthought, asked the boy his name.

"My name is like yours, sir," the youth stammered. "It's Alexander!"

The general was suddenly enraged. He grabbed the young man and yanked him to his feet. "Now hear me," he growled, glaring directly into the youth's eyes. "Either change your ways or change your name!"[25]

Think what would happen if hundreds of thousands — millions? — of parents decided to live radically, assuming responsibility for the education of their children, curtailing the pervasive influence of television, working in concert with like-minded families in the community to raise a generation of young people in the fear and admonition of the Lord, teaching them that it is not wrong to be different, then sending them out into the world to reclaim for their children what has been lost by default.

As David Mains says, "The people who bear the name of Christ are in the thick of a battle of cosmic proportions, under the leadership of the Great Commander-in-Chief, who is also our Father. As members of His family, we bear His divine name, *children of God.*"

And God says:

Either change your ways or change your name.

ENDNOTES

Preface

1. Tim LaHaye, *Faith of Our Founding Fathers* (Brentwood, TN: Wolgemuth and Hyatt, 1987), p. 1.
2. John Goodlad, "Learning and Teaching in the Future," *NEA Journal,* 1968. Cited in Charlotte T. Iserbyt, *Wolves in Sheep's Clothing* (Des Moines: Conscience Press, 1995), p. 7.
3. Al Gore, *Earth in the Balance* (Boston: Houghton Mifflin Co., 1992).
4. Charlotte T. Iserbyt, *Wolves in Sheep's Clothing,* (Des Moines: Conscience Press, 1995), p. 8.
5. Ibid.
6. Ibid.
7. Ibid.
8. Samuel L. Blumenfeld, *NEA: Trojan Horse in American Education* (Boise, ID: The Paradigm Company, 1984).
9. Peter Brimelow and Leslie Spencer, "The National Extortion Association," *Forbes Magazine,* 1993.
10. Iserbyt, *Wolves in Sheep's Clothing,* p. 11.

Introduction

1. Dr. Jack Kevorkian, speaking at the National Press Club, July 29, 1996.

2. Dr. John A Huffman, Sr. From a sermon preached July 11, 1995, St. Andrew's Presbyterian Church, Newport Beach, CA.
3. American Family Association, Tupelo, Mississippi, August 1997.
4. George Grant, *The Family Under Siege* (Minneapolis, MN: Bethany House Publishers, 1994), p. 88.
5. William J. Bennett, *The Devaluing of America* (New York: Summit Books, 1994), p. 254.

1. A Walk Down 16th Street

1. Charles Claude Selecman, *The Methodist Primer* (Nashville, TN: Nashville Tidings, 1944, 1948)
2. Mark Tooley, "Homosexual Celebration at President Clinton's Church," *American Family Association Journal*, February 1996.
3. Ibid.
4. Homer L. Calkin, *Castings From the Foundry Mold* (Pearl River, NY: Parthenon Press, 1968), p. 135.
5. Ibid.
6. Robert E. Coleman, *Nothing To Do But To Save Souls* (Grand Rapids, MI: Francis Asbury Press, 1990), p. 100.
7. George Grant, *The Family Under Siege*, p. 77.
8. Ibid.
9. Ibid.
10. Ibid., p. 78.
11. Ibid., p. 75.
12. James R. Patrick, *Research Manual*, Citizens for Academic Excellence, 1994.
13. Bennett, *The Devaluing of America*.
14. Grant, *The Family Under Siege*.
15. Ibid.

16. National Education Association Headquarters, Washington, D.C.
17. Linda Chavez, "Where's Our Moral Outrage?" *USA Today*, Sept. 11, 1996.
18. Ibid.
19. "Shame Shame: Trading on Infamy," *Chicago Tribune*, Oct. 11, 1996.
20. Grant, The Family Under Siege.
21. Ibid.
22. Ibid.
23. Ibid.
24. Carol Everett, "The Oppression of Choice," *Reclaiming America for Christ* (Fort Lauderdale, FL: Coral Ridge Ministries, 1996).
25. Grant, *The Family Under Siege*.
26. Robert H. Bork, *Slouching Towards Gomorrah* (New York: Regan Books, 1996).
27. Maureen Dowd, "The Man in the Mirror," *The New York Times*, 1996.

2. The Decade of Decision

1. Cal Thomas, "The Sixties Are Dead: Long Live the Nineties," *Imprimis*, 1995.
2. Ibid.
3. Ibid.
4. Bork, *Slouching Towards Gomorrah*.
5. Ibid.
6. Ibid.
7. Ibid.
8. Ibid.
9. Genesis 1:27.
10. Cal Thomas, "The Sixties Are Dead."

11. Ibid.
12. Herbert London, "Remember Moral Absolutes?" *The Washington Times*, Nov. 24, 1996.
13. Ibid.
14. Bork, *Slouching Towards Gomorrah.*
15. John Silber, *Straight Shooting* (New York, NY: Harper Perennial, 1989).
16. Allan Bloom, *The Closing of the American Mind* (New York: Simon & Shuster, 1987).
17. Bork, *Slouching Towards Gomorrah.*
18. Ibid.
19. George Roche, *The Fall of the Ivory Tower* (Washington, D.C.: Regnery Publishing, 1994).
20. Ibid.
21. Ibid.
22. Ibid.
23. Ibid.
24. *Comedy and Tragedy*, A Survey Compiled and Published by Young America's Foundation, 1996.
25. Ibid.

3. Barbarians in the City

1. James Montgomery Boice, *Two Cities, Two Loves* (Downers Grove, IL: InterVarsity Press, 1996).
2. Charles Colson with Ellen Santilli Vaughn, *Against the Night: Living in the New Dark Ages* (Ann Arbor, MI: Servant, 1989).
3. *Family Voice*, Concerned Women of America.
4. Colson, *Against the Night.*
5. *USA Today*, Sept. 23, 1996.
6. John J. Vitulio, Jr., "Community Policing: Can It Cut Crime?" Policy Research Institute, Nov. 1997.

7. Mona Charen, "Moral Confusion in Bill Clinton's America," *The Washington Times*, Dec. 8, 1996.

8. Brenda Hunter, "Attachment and Infant Daycare," *Who Will Rock the Cradle?* (Dallas, TX: Word Publishing, 1989).

9. Raymond S. Moore, "Home Grown Children Have the Advantage," *Who Will Rock the Cradle?* (Dallas, TX: Word Publishing, 1989).

10. Rosaline Bush, *Family Voice*, Feb. 1997.

11. Lee Moriwaki, "Church Reflects SF's Tenderloin," *The Seattle Times*, Oct. 13, 1984.

12. E. Earle Ellis, *Paul's Attitude to Scripture*.

13. Boice, *Two Cities, Two Loves*.

14. *Minneapolis Star Tribune*, April 12, 1996.

15. CNN Interview, June 1997.

16. Rev. Dale Turner, "Fundamentalism — It Sees Bible Narrowly With Admirable Fervor," *The Seattle Times*, Nov. 26, 1988.

17. Meg Greenfield, *Newsweek*.

18. *Church of the Holy Trinity vs. United States* (143 UA457, 36L ed. 226). Supreme Court, 1891.

19. Tal Brooke, *America's Waning Light: The Betrayal of Our Christian Heritage* (Chicago: Moody Press, 1994).

20. Ibid.

21. Boice, *Two Cities, Two Loves*.

22. Christian Hoff Sommers, "How to Teach Right and Wrong," *Christianity Today*, Dec. 13, 1993.

23. Ibid.

24. Silber, *Straight Shooting*.

25. Cal Thomas, The New Challenge: Avoiding Media Distractions," *The Washington Times*, Nov. 28, 1994.

26. Erwin W. Lutzer, *Hitler's Cross* (Chicago: Moody Press, 1995).

27. George Roche, *A World Without Heroes: The Modern Tragedy* (Hillsdale, MI: Hillsdale College Press, 1987).
28. Lutzer, *Hitler's Cross.*
29. Ibid.
30. Elie Wiesel, From the Kingdom of Memory, Summit Books, 1990.
31. Lutzer, *Hitler's Cross.*
32. Ibid.
33. Rosell K. Chartock and Jack Spencer, *Can It Happen Again?* (New York, NY: Black Dog and Leventhal, 1995).

4. Sights and Sounds of Decadence

1. Michael A. Lerner, "The Heavy-Metal Frenzy," *Newsweek,* Aug. 10, 1987.
2. Bork, *Slouching Towards Gomorrah.*
3. Ibid.
4. Ibid.
5. Allan Bloom, *The Closing of the American Mind.*
6. E. Lonnie Melashenko, *The Television Time Bomb* (Boise, ID: Pacific Press Publishing Assoc., 1993).
7. Silber, *Straight Shooting.*
8. Ibid.
9. Ibid.
10. Ibid.
11. David R. Mains, *The Rise of the Religion of Antichristism* (Grand Rapids, MI: Zondervan Publishing House, 1985).
12. Jeffrey Hart, "Educate Your Child; Turn Off the TV," *The Washington Times,* Aug. 14, 1996.
13. Ibid.

14. B. Russell Holt, "Amusing Ourselves to Death," *Ministry Magazine*, Nov. 1986.
15. Silber, *Straight Shooting*.
16. Michael Coren, *The Man Who Created Narnia* (Grand Rapids, MI: Eerdmans, 1994).
17. Rosemary Cari Benet, "Nancy Hanks," Prose and Poetry of America (Syracuse, NY: L. W. Singer Co., 1994).

5. The "Magic" of Sex Education

1. Derrich Z. Jackson, *The Sunday Boston Globe*, Nov. 10, 1991.
2. Earvin "Magic" Johnson, *What You Can Do to Avoid AIDS* (Times Books, 1992).
3. Ibid.
4. Lynne S. Dumas, *Talking With Kids About Tough Issues*, Henry J. Kaiser Foundation.
5. Ibid.
6. Richard A. Knox, *The Sunday Boston Globe*, Nov. 10, 1991.
7. Barbara Reynolds, "From the Heart," *USA Today*, Nov. 15, 1991.
8. Anna Quindlen, "Believe in Magic," *The New York Times*, Nov. 9, 1991.
9. Ibid.
10. James Dobson and Gary L. Bauer, *Children at Risk* (Dallas, TX: Word Publishing, 1990).
11. Ibid.
12. Ibid.
13. Ibid.
14. Ibid.

15. Cal Thomas, "America's Slide into Self-Destruction," *The Washington Times*, June 24, 1995.
16. Patrick Sandoval, "Abstinence Only Is Not Reality-Based," *The Denver Post*, Sept. 24, 1994.
17. Jana Mazanec, "Birth Rate Soars At Colorado Schools," *USA Today*, May 19, 1992.
18. Sandoval, "Abstinence Only."
19. J. D. Unwin, *Sex and Culture*, 1934.
20. Silber, *Straight Shooting*.

6. America's Saddest Day

1. Jane H. Ingraham, "Is Public Education Necessary?" *The New American*, Oct. 13, 1996.
2. Ibid.
3. Elmer Towns, *Has Public Education "Had It"?* (Nashville, TN: Thomas Nelson, 1974).
4. Cathy Duffy, *Government Nannies* (Gresham, OR: Noble Publishing, 1995).
5. Ibid.
6. Ron Sunseri, *Outcome Based Education* (Seattle, WA: Questar Publishers, 1994).
7. Grant, *The Family Under Siege.*
8. Ibid.
9. Duffy, *Government Nannies.*
10. Ibid.
11. Ibid.
12. Clarence B. Carson, *A Basic History of the United States* (American Textbook Commission, 1985).
13. Ibid.
14. Ibid.
15. Duffy, *Government Nannies.*
16. Ibid.

17. Ibid.
18. Ibid.

7. Conflict in the Classroom

1. John Dunphy, *The Humanist Magazine*, Jan./Feb.1983.
2. Carson, *A Basic History of the United States, Vol. 3* (American Textbook Commission, 1985).
3. Silber, *Straight Shooting*.
4. Towns, *Has Public Education "Had It"?*
5. Ibid.
6. Ibid.
7. Ibid.
8. Ibid.
9. Dennis L. Cuddy, Ph.D., *Chronology of Education*, Pro-Family Forum, Inc., 1994.
10. Duffy, *Government Nannies*.
11. Debbie Cafazzo, "School Reform Ready For Its First Real Test," *The News Tribune, March 23, 1997*.
12. *Charles J. Sykes, Dumbing Down Our Kids* (New York: St. Martin's Press, 1995).
13. Ibid.
14. Towns, *Has Public Education "Had It"?*
15. William F. Buckley, Jr., "Public Schools Turned into Citadels for Special Interests, Not Education," *Pittsburgh Tribune Review, June 29, 1997*.
16. Cathy Duffy, *Government Nannies*.
17. Silber, *Straight Shooting*.

8. The NEA: Humanism's Ally

1. "Recognizing the Radical Right," Prepared by Minnesota Education Association Center for Public Education Advocacy, Feb. 10-11, 1995.

2. Ibid.
3. Towns, *Has Public Education "Had It"?*
4. Ibid.
5. *The Humanist Manifesto*, 1973.
6. Cuddy, *Chronology of Education.*
7. Ibid.
8. Berit Kjos, *Brave New Schools* (Eugene, OR: Harvest House, 1995).
9. Sidney Hook, *The Humanist Manifesto*, 1997.
10. Paul Blanchard, *The Humanist Manifesto*, 1976.
11. *The Humanist Manifesto*, 1973.
12. Grant, *The Family Under Siege.*
13. Ibid.
14. Buckley, "Public Schools Turned into Citadels . . ."
15. NEA Headquarters, Washington, D.C.
16. *The NEA Journal*, 1955.
17. Berit Kjos, *Brave New Schools.*
18. Towns, *Has Public Education "Had It"?*
19. Ibid.
20. David Harmer, *School Choice*, CATO Institute, 1994.
21. Alexis de Tocqueville, *Democracy in America*, The New American Library, 1956.

9. Outcomes or Lost Opportunities?

1. Sunseri, *Outcome Based Education.*
2. Phyllis Schlafley, *The Phyllis Schlafley Report*, The Eagle Trust Fund, May 1993.
3. Sunseri, *Outcome Based Education.*
4. Phyllis Schlafley, *The Phyllis Schlafley Report.*
5. Dana Mack, *The Assault on Parenthood* (New York: Simon & Shuster, 1997).
6. Phyllis Schlafley, *The Phyllis Schlafley Report.*

7. Sunseri, *Outcome Based Education*.
8. Ibid.
9. Mack, *The Assault on Parenthood*.
10. Dennis L. Cuddy, Ph.D., *Chronology of Education*, Pro-Family Forum, Inc., 1994.
11. Sunseri, *Outcome Based Education*.
12. Ibid.
13. Ibid.
14. Ibid.
15. Ibid.
16. Ibid.
17. James R. Patrick, *Research Manual*.
18. Dennis L. Cuddy, Ph.D., *Chronology of Education*.
19. Ibid.
20. Personal letter dated Aug. 11, 1997.
21. Ron Sunseri, *Outcome Based Education*.
22. Ibid.
23. Ibid.
24. Personal 18-page letter from Marc Tucker, President of National Center of Education and Economy, to Hillary Clinton.
25. Ibid.
26. Learning a Living, U.S. Dept. of Labor, 1992, p. 61, from Pam Hoffecker.
27. The New York Times, March 26, 1992.
28. Dennis L. Cuddy, Ph.D., *Chronology of Education*.
29. Phyllis Schlafley, *The Phyllis Schlafley Report*.

10. The Road to Nowhere

1. Walter Williams, "Blacks Victimized by Malpractice of Education Establishment in U.S," *Pittsburgh Tribune Review*, July 30, 1997.

2. Samuel L. Blumenfeld, *The New Illiterates* (Boise, ID: The Paradigm Company).
3. Williams, "Blacks Victimized."
4. Blumenfeld, *NEA: Trojan Horse in American Education,* p. 104.
5. Ibid.
6. Ibid., p. 105.
7. Ibid.
8. Ibid., p. 121.
9. Ibid., p. 107.
10. Ibid., p. 114.
11. Ibid., p. 119.
12. Walter Williams, "Blacks Victimized."
13. Dr. D. James Kennedy, *Reclaiming America for Christ* (Fort Lauderdale, FL: Coral Ridge Ministries, 1996), p. 200.
14. Ibid.
15. Ibid., p. 201.
16. Ibid., p. 202.
17. Ibid..
18. Ibid.
19. Ibid., p. 206.
20. Ibid.
21. Cited in Sykes, *Dumbing Down Our Kids,* p. 21.
22. Ibid., p. 97.
23. Ibid.
24. Ibid., p. 101.
25. Ibid.
26. Ibid., p. 102.

11. A World Within the World

1. Bork, *Slouching Towards Gomorrah,* p. 12.
2. Ibid.

3. Father Patrick W. Egan, "Goodbye, Father O'Malley," *Pastoral Renewal,* July/August 1985.

4. Phyllis Schlafley, *Who Will Rock the Cradle?* (Dallas, TX: Word Publishers, 1989), p. 123.

5. *Heritage Foundation Issue Bulletin.*

6. Mack, *The Assault on Parenthood,* p. 29.

7. Cited in Schlafley, *Who Will Rock the Cradle?,* p. 85.

8. Michael P. Farris, "The Solid Evidence to Support Home Schooling," *The Wall Street Journal,* March 5, 1997.

9. Ibid.

10. Ibid.

11. Arianna Huffington, "Washington Displays Ignorance When Subject Turns to Education," *Pittsburgh Tribune Review,* Aug. 1, 1997.

12. Cited in *Reclaiming America for Christ* (Fort Lauderdale, FL: Coral Ridge Ministries, 1996), p. 191.

13. Mark Noll, *The Scandal of the Evangelical Mind* (Grand Rapids. MI: Eerdmans, 1994), p. 3.

14. Os Guinness, *Fit Bodies Fit Minds* (Grand Rapids, MI: Baker Books, 1994).

15. Melashenko, *The Television Time Bomb,* p. 60.

16. Karl Menninger, M.D., *Whatever Became of Sin?* (New York: Bantam Books, 1973), p. 229.

17. J. Alan Peterson, *Run With the Horses* (Downers Grove, IL: InterVarsity Press, 1983), p. 11.

18. Ibid.

19. Ibid.

20. Melashenko, *The Television Time Bomb,* p. 61.

21. Cal Thomas, "Critics are Missing Something," *The Washington Times,* July, 1997.

22. David McCullough, "The Unexpected Mrs. Stowe," *Brave Companions* (New York: Simon & Schuster, 1992), p. 37.
23. Ibid.
24. Bill Sanders, *School Daze* (Tarrytown, NY: Flemming H. Revell, 1992), p. 64.
25. David Mains, *The Rise of . . . Antichristism,* p. 127.

WHAT AMERICAN CULTURAL LEADERS ARE SAYING ABOUT

Come Home America . . .

It was a pleasure meeting you and listening to your message at the First Assembly of God Church in Green Bay recently. I have also enjoyed your book, *Come Home America,* in which you have so ably identified our nation's denial of God and gradual descent from family structure.

This descent has seen good people in this country rationalize heretofore unacceptable behavior as appropriate, and our hope of reversing this trend rests in the efforts of people like you to set the record straight. God bless you, and best of luck in your mission to reestablish our country's foundation.

PAUL F. JADIN, MAYOR
Green Bay, Wisconsin

Come Home America is the title of a new book by Daniel E. Johnson. It questions how the United States "went wrong.". . . When he addressed the '72 Democratic National Convention as presidential nominee, McGovern called for U.S. troops to return from the Vietnam War with his cry: "Come Home, America!" The slogan was much derided by Republicans. Noting the Johnson book, Democratic political consultant and former McGovern aide Robert Schrum commented dryly: "I knew George would become a consensus national figure some day."

ROBERT NOVAK, COLUMNIST
New York Post

You and I may not agree on all political points, but I certainly appreciate the generosity and kindness of your letter, and I wish you well in all of your efforts. At least you and I have in common being criticized by Robert Novak!

GEORGE MCGOVERN, FORMER SENATOR
1972 Presidential Candidate

Your book is a classic . . . a shocker! . . . I would tell people: If you don't want to lose your temper or a night's sleep, if you don't want to be driven to your knees in prayer or shed tears for America, don't read Dan Johnson's *Come Home America*. It stirs and disturbs, it jars the mind and wrenches the soul. . . .

DR. PAUL LOWENBERG, PREACHER
Former Church Executive

I just received a copy of your new book. I can see that it's a winner.

MELVIN E. BEYER, ATTORNEY

The information in *Come Home America* is powerful and without question a great resource to this ministry. You are to be commended for the hard work and hours of research that you have put into this book.

SAMUEL RIJFKOGEL, EVANGELIST

I am grateful for the copy of your new book. . . . I
admire the quality which has earmarked all of your
accomplishments for our Master. Your diligent
striving for excellence has been an inspiration for me
and many others who have admired you from afar.

> DON GEORGE, PASTOR
> Irving, Texas

Thank you for your latest book, *Come Home America.*
. . . The information you have covered is timely and
insightful. I am sure it will be a resource as I prepare
my sermon for our congregation's July 4th celebration. . . . Your book is a valuable tool for research and
reference.

> EARL J. BANNING, PASTOR
> Houston, Texas

Dan Johnson has written an accurate and poignant
account of American moral decline. Like the ancient
prophet, he details in *Come Home America* what it will
take to right the course.

> RICH WILKERSON, EVANGELIST

The theme is timely . . . and prescribes what is
needed to bring our country back to its greatness.

> JAMES BLACKWOOD, GOSPEL SINGER

It's always a joy to "Come Home!" There is safety
and peace "at home." Daniel Johnson has struck a

chord that resonates from coast to coast in *Come Home America*. Read it and hope!

DR. GLEN D. COLE, SUPERINTENDENT
Northern California Assemblies of God

Your little brother Sam gave me a copy of your great book, *Come Home America*. I have read it through and couldn't put it down. This book is long overdue. It is a masterpiece.

DWAIN JONES, REPRESENTATIVE
Mission of Mercy

Speaking Engagements

Dan Johnson is available for speaking engagements
for churches, conferences, and schools.

For further information, contact:

Daniel E. Johnson
P.O. Box 42460
Tacoma, WA 98442
USA
1-800-216-4333

For information on *Aim for the Children,*
or other books and tapes by Dan Johnson,
write to the above address or fax:

(253) 474-2564